SPORTS CARS

James Mann

motorbooks

First published in 2011 by Motorbooks, an imprint of Quarto Publishing Group USA Inc., 400 First Avenue North, Suite 400, Minneapolis, MN 55401 USA

Motorbooks titles are also available at discounts in bulk quantity for industrial or sales-promotional use. For details write to Special Sales Manager at Quarto Publishing Group USA Inc., 400 First Avenue North, Suite 400, Minneapolis, MN 55401 USA.

To find out more about our books, visit us online at www.motorbooks.com.

ISBN-13: 978-0-7603-4028-8

4 5 6

Editors: Jeffrey Zuehlke
Design Manager: Kou Lor
Layout by: Kazuko Collins
Cover design: Matthew Simmons

Printed in China

On the front cover: Porsche Boxster

On the frontis: Triumph TR2

On the title page: Riley Imp

On the back cover, top: Lamborghini Miura;
Center: Chevrolet Corvette Sting Ray;
Bottom: Triumph TR3A

CONTENTS

ACKNOWLEDGMENTS

Many thanks to the people who helped me with information for this book, particularly Tom Falconer for his infallible Corvette knowledge and Mick Walsh, Alistair Clements, and James Elliott from *Classic and Sports Car* magazine, who answered my often-daft questions without complaint, and Tim Bulley who allowed the use of the TR6 and Riley Imp images.

DK Engineering for the use of their Ferrari
    California
Holly Robinson in the Audi press office for
    supplying the TT
Gian Avignone at Tesla Motors
Kevin Watters at Aston Martin
Paul Matty Sports Cars for the Elan Sprint, Elise,
    and Esprit S4
Mike Rolls for the MGB

And the owners:
Gilbert and Anna East, Mazda MX-5 Mk.1
Allan and Joy Legg, Mazda MX-5 Mk.3.5
Bob and Jill Lock, Morgan Three-Wheeler
Derek Richards, Morgan Plus 4
Nick Moody, Morgan Plus 4
Jim Dean, MGA
Paul Smith, Dodge Viper
Mike Lake, TR3A
Robert Sackey, TR4A
Guy Portlock, smart roadster
Robin Stainer, AC Cobra
Hal Bonhe, Austin-Healey Sprite
Simon Box, Honda S2000

And the clubs:
Morgan Three-Wheeler Club
Morgan Club
MG Car Club
TR Register
MG Owners' Club

INTRODUCTION

As soon as the very first car was invented over 120 years ago, people have found ways to make them go faster, round corners better, and look more beautiful than the car next door.

The definition of a sports car is not straightforward—two seats, rear-wheel drive, and a racy motor don't begin to describe the genre. It's hard to put your finger on what defines a sports car because it is not a logical definition. Is it a car that's fun to drive, a car one wants to drive just for the sake of driving? Or is it the kind of machine that inspires the passion to painstakingly restore it to its original luster?

No, we've evolved a totally illogical, emotional relationship with these hunks of wood, steel, and leather because of competition—competition for a girl or guy, competition for speed, or competition for the prestige and glamour that the ultimate automotive consumable can offer its owner. It's a base instinct—and the carmakers know it—a desire that we all somehow want to be one-up on the next guy (or gal). Sports cars tempt us with sleek lines and powerful motors, and sell their styles to us just to satisfy a need.

The sheer dullness and competency of many modern cars has sparked an ever-increasing interest in sports cars, for if the journey is to be done, why not have fun doing it? So a sports car must have a balance of power turned into speed and acceleration and handling. There is nothing more unsettling or dangerous than a vehicle with high performance in a straight line and bad handling in the corners; yet a relative lack of performance can be somewhat mitigated by sweet handling.

The birth of the sports car truly came about when the car manufacturers realized that by making race cars for the road, they could sell their products using the excitement of speed and the glamor of the track and its heroic drivers. Before World War II, such cars were very exclusive: A car such as the Bugatti Type 35—one you could drive to a track, race, and drive home again—was beyond the dreams of most ordinary folk, but it was the reality for the few, and that was enough. Those prewar sports cars were often hand-built, with low production runs of tens or a few hundred cars, and owners had to put up with leaky, cramped, uncomfortable cabins and dangerously inadequate brakes. Styling at the time was more varied than the homogenized CAD designs of today with ranges of cars that reflected national identities. You could tell a Ford from an Austin or a Mercedes from a Bentley without having to look at the badge.

After World War II, scores of GIs returned home to the United States with tales of nippy little British sports cars, and some of them brought the cars home with them, paying valuable dollars to the struggling U.K. economy and beginning a special relationship that would last for decades. And so a generation of smaller and more affordable sporty cars began to appear, offering the joy of driving to a wider audience.

At the same time, carmakers began to see how the relatively small sales numbers of these nimble machines was more than made up for by their charisma. They helped to sell the more mundane models in their ranges. For example, the boss of Austin knew a good thing when he saw it, and he saw it at the 1952 Earl's Court Motor Show in the fast-looking Healey 100. He secured a deal with the car's maker, Donald Healey, there and then to build the sports car under the Austin-Healey badge. In the 1960s, Ford built and raced the fabulous GT40, which helped to sell Thunderbirds and Mustangs as well as all the other family cars in Ford's model line.

MG conscientiously developed its brand to emote something special with its "Safety Fast" slogan, although its cars were not particularly innovative or even that fast. Boss Cecil Kimber understood that an element of snobbery existed that could be capitalized on to sell his sports cars all over the world.

Some of the best-loved sports cars were developed from the competition departments of BMC, Jaguar, and Lotus—not to mention Ferrari—all of which poured millions of dollars into their race programs over the decades. And once a racing reputation was established, such as with Jaguar C- and D-types, the company could sell all the E-types it could make without having to race another car. Racing also brought many new engineering advances to the sports car, such as disc brakes, low-slung chassis, supercharging, and tire technology.

The swinging '60s created the ideal breeding ground for the sports car with new ideas, fashions, hopes, and freedoms to enjoy. Sports cars appeared in movies, and rock-and-roll bands sang about their XKEs, Sting Rays, and getting their kicks on Route 66. So the sports car became a glamorous marketing tool to make other, more ordinary, styles more attractive under the same badge. It harkened back to the days of cheap fuel, empty roads before gridlock, and no speed limits—the sports car brought back the days when driving was pure pleasure.

But it wasn't to last. In the 1970s, strict new safety legislation and emission controls put an end to many of the imports into the United States and the market became more motivated toward hot hatches and GTs. It took a fairly small Japanese carmaker to wake up the market again in the 1990s with the fantastic MX-5 Miata. All of a sudden, sports cars were back with a rash of other exciting new models like the Lotus Elise, Porsche Boxster, and Honda S2000.

The sports car, however, is without a doubt a luxury product—very few of us sports car owners use them as everyday cars. And with just two seats and their gas-guzzling motors destroying the planet (at least, according to the anti-automobile lobby), some think their days may be numbered. But as long as people have a desire to own a fast car that is fun to drive, the spirit of the sports car will prevail, perhaps in ways we can only imagine today.

CHAPTER 1
VINTAGE SPORTS CARS

We often use the term "vintage" to refer to old cars, but in truth vintage cars are those built in the years between the world wars, 1918 through 1939. It was one of richest periods of sports car building and racing, with hundreds of manufacturers competing for a slice of the action. Many of the names are long gone but a few are familiar.

Bentley, founded in 1919 by Walter Owen (W. O.) Bentley, made enormous luxury leviathans that cost as much as a small country estate. Morgan, Riley, and Austin served the common man. And yet all sporting builders shared a common desire to make cars that could go faster around corners. Enzo Ferrari, who ran the works racing team for Alfa Romeo, said Bentley's cars were like trucks compared his finely engineered Italian thoroughbreds. It was a fair comparison, perhaps, but such limitations didn't stop Bentleys from winning many, many sports car races.

The manufacturers of this era were the first to see that competition success led to showroom sales. Many sports cars were as good on the race circuit as they were on the road. In fact, it was not uncommon for a competitor in a sports car race to drive to the track, race, and drive home again afterward. Unlike drivers of purpose-built single-seaters, sports car owners could see a direct correlation between the cars they drove and the models racing around the tracks.

The much-admired BMW 328 was a great all-rounder, with its sweeping body lines and superb sporty motor. BMW campaigned the model in rallies as well as races, winning the 1939 RAC Rally and achieving a class win in the great Italian road race, the 1,000-mile Mille Miglia. It is also the only car on our vintage list to be offered in coupe version with a roof—quite a luxury in the pared-down, Spartan world of prewar sports cars.

The 1750 is the ultimate 1930s sports car in terms of performance, style, and price. Alfa Romeo supplied chassis and its superb straight-six dual-overhead-cam (DOHC) engine. The body was then added, usually by Zagato, although the body of the car pictured below was added by British coachbuilder Freestone and Webb, a firm that was more commonly associated with Bentley. The car on page 14 is a Zagato body.

On the racetrack, Alfa had scored great success with its supercharged P2 racer, which had been masterminded by ex-Fiat engineer Vittorio Jano. It was the supercharger that made

ALFA ROMEO 1750 GT SPYDER

Country of manufacture: Italy
Years of production: 1929–1933
Engine: 1,750cc DOHC straight six
Output: 85 horsepower
Top speed: 95 miles per hour
Number built: 369

the light, short-chassis Alfa Romeo special, giving real power to its low-compression, high-revving engine. The P2 became the staple competition car of the period, winning everything from the Mille Miglia to the

24-hour race at Spa. Motorsports success meant road car sales, making Alfa Romeo a serious contender in the sports car market.

Suspension on the 1750 was by way of solid front and live rear axle, with semi-elliptical leaf springs and drum brakes all around. Under the bonnet, the Roots-type supercharger featured an alloy intake manifold finned for lightness and cooling, ideas developed from the race cars. The 1750 introduced the term *gran turismo* (GT) to motoring vocabulary and can be described as the ancestor of every sports car today, with its aerodynamic lines, simple suspension, and finely engineered motor.

Did You Know?

Alfa Romeo fielded four 1750s for the 1930 Mille Miglia, which came down to an epic duel between rival Alfa drivers Tazio Nuvolari and Achille Varzi. Legend has it that in the predawn hours of the race, the trailing Nuvolari turned off his headlights as he approached an unwary Varzi. Then, as he made his move, Nuvolari snapped on his lights and roared past his stunned rival on his way to victory.

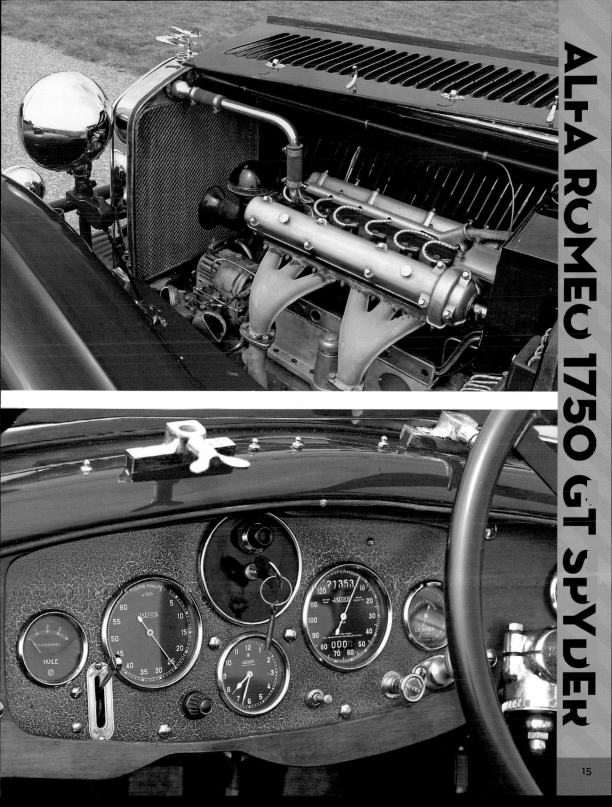

With flowing wings and a shortened tail housing the spare wheel, the Riley Imp was one of the best-looking small sports cars of the 1930s. The Imp was a sporty development of the successful Riley Nine, and both models featured Riley's fantastic engine—a lightweight four-cylinder water-cooled unit with twin, low-set camshafts operating short pushrods

RILEY IMP

Country of manufacture: U.K.
Years of production: 1934–1935
Engine: 1,087cc overhead valve inline four-cylinder
Output: 50 horsepower
Top speed: 75 miles per hour
Number built: 75

and overhead valves. A pair of SU carburetors provided fuel to highly advanced hemispherical cross-flow cylinder heads. The setup delivered world-beating performance in its 1,087cc class.

In the Imp, the chassis was upswept over the front axle and underslung at the rear, as in the highly successful Riley Brooklands race car—the land speed record–holder at the time—developed by engineer-racers Reid Railton and J. G. Parry-Thomas. The Imp came with either a four-speed manual transmission or a pre-selector gearbox, which allowed the driver to choose his next gear and engage it when he dipped the clutch in a single fast action, saving any need for double de-clutching. Stopping power came via cable-operated drum brakes all around.

The 4-½-liter blown (supercharged) Bentleys, or Blower Bentleys, were the supercars of their day—expensive, astonishingly fast, not very reliable, and extraordinarily fuel-hungry, achieving just 2.8 miles per gallon. The original 4 ½ was a development of the successful 3-liter car that had won the 24 Hours of Le Mans race in 1924. It shared the same simple chassis with four-wheel brakes and semi-elliptical suspension, but the 4 ½'s four-cylinder block was bored out 100mm in the racing models, increasing the engine's output to a very muscular (for the era) 130 horsepower.

BENTLEY 4-½-LITER SUPERCHARGED

Country of manufacture: U.K.
Years of production: 1929–1930
Engine: 4,398cc supercharged inline four-cylinder
Output: 175 horsepower
Top speed: over 100 miles per hour
Number built: 55

The formula worked, helping to propel a 4 ½ to victory at Le Mans again in 1928. But this would prove to be the Bentley's limit, at

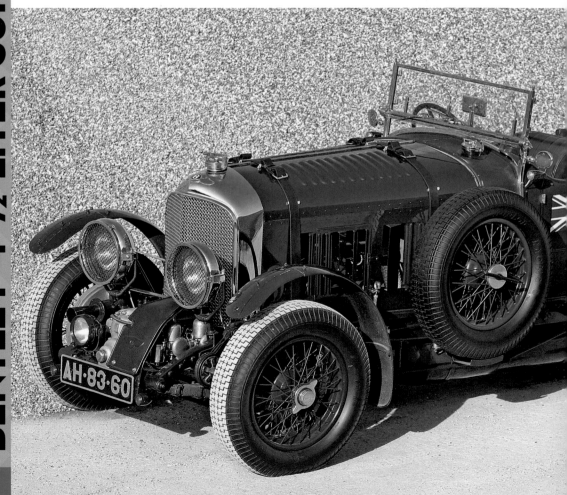

least in normally aspirated form. Sir Henry "Tim" Birkin, one of the now-famous "Bentley Boy" gentleman racers, proposed adding a supercharger to boost performance. Walter Owen Bentley was not a fan of superchargers and famously said, "There's no replacement for displacement." He stuck to his guns and produced the Speed 6, a 6-½-liter car that would win Le Mans glory in 1929 and 1930.

Meanwhile, Birkin went ahead and brought in engineer Amherst Villiers to build the supercharger, which stuck out of the front of the car, fed by two huge SU carburetors. In 1932, one of Birkin's blown 4 ½s was tested around the banked circuit at Brooklands, where it achieved a speed of 137.96 miles per hour.

Did You Know?
Legendary British secret agent James Bond drove a 4-½-liter Blower Bentley in Ian Fleming's first three 007 novels—*Casino Royale* (1953), *Live and Let Die* (1954), and *Moonraker* (1955).

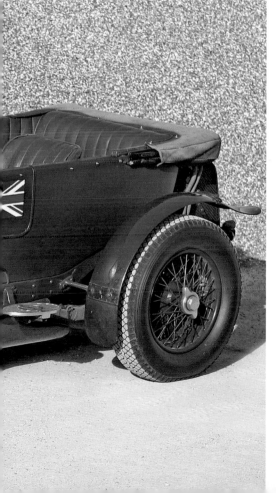

Although named a replica, the car seen here is not a duplicate of a particular model. It's a celebration of the cars that competed in the Tourist Trophy race on the Ards road circuit in Northern Ireland in the 1930s.

Captain Archie Frazer Nash had been making cars for years, but he was not a good businessman and nearly went bankrupt in 1929. He was saved by the Aldington family, the brothers who saw the potential of Archie's light, nimble sports cars. They set about building the brand with clever marketing, naming each new model to capitalize on the company's competition successes.

One of the quirks of the Frazer Nash cars was the chain drive, which produced quick changes and saved the weight of a heavy gearbox. The drive design utilized a dog clutch and bevel box, providing four speeds. With its solid rear axle, the car was simple and cheap to build.
The basic engine was an overhead-cam straight four designed by Albert Gough for Frazer Nash.

TTs were also built with either a six-cylinder Blackburne or Meadows engine.

Gough's motor was the best, especially when fitted with a supercharger. The cars were highly successful in competition, particularly the extremely tough Alpine Trials. This car was entered for the 1935 running of the 24 Hours of Le Mans and, as a warmup, competed at the famous Brooklands banked circuit near London, where these pictures were taken.

FRAZER NASH TT REPLICA

Country of manufacture: U.K.
Year of production: 1934
Engine: 1,496cc overhead-cam inline four-cylinder
Output: 55 horsepower
Top speed: 80 miles per hour
Number built: 83

Did You Know?

Frazer Nash still produces cars today. Its Namir model is the fastest hybrid-electric car in the world, with a top speed of 187 miles per hour.

FRAZER NASH TT REPLICA

BMP 846

After just seven years of making automobiles, aircraft- and motorcycle-maker BMW produced a remarkable car in the 328. It was fast, stylish, and expensive, costing twice as much as a family sedan. The 328 featured a powerful six-cylinder, overhead-valve engine with three down-draft carburetors, "hemi" heads to improve performance, and unorthodox transverse pushrods driven by a single camshaft—the brainchild of BMW's technical director, Fritz Fiedler.

BMW 328

Country of manufacture: Germany
Years of production: 1936–1939
Engine: 1,971cc overhead-valve inline six-cylinder
Output: 80 horsepower
Top speed: 100 miles per hour
Number built: 464

The body and frame were an evolution of the BMW 319's tubular chassis, considerably lightened and stiffened in order to compete in

the lucrative 2-liter sports car class. The 328's unique cowled-in headlamps added to its streamlined shape. It also featured hydraulic brakes, independent front suspension, and rack and pinion steering, which gave superb road-holding and cornering ability rarely experienced before in a production sports car.

Straight away, it proved successful in competition, winning the prestigious Eifelrennen race at the Nürburgring in Germany, ahead of the more powerful Alfa Romeos. The 328 also performed well in standard guise in the 1938 Mille Miglia. World War II deprived the car of further victories, but 328s continued to compete for another 10 years postwar and inspired a brave new wave of sports car designers.

Did You Know?
The BMW badge hails back to the company's aircraft days and represents a turning propeller.

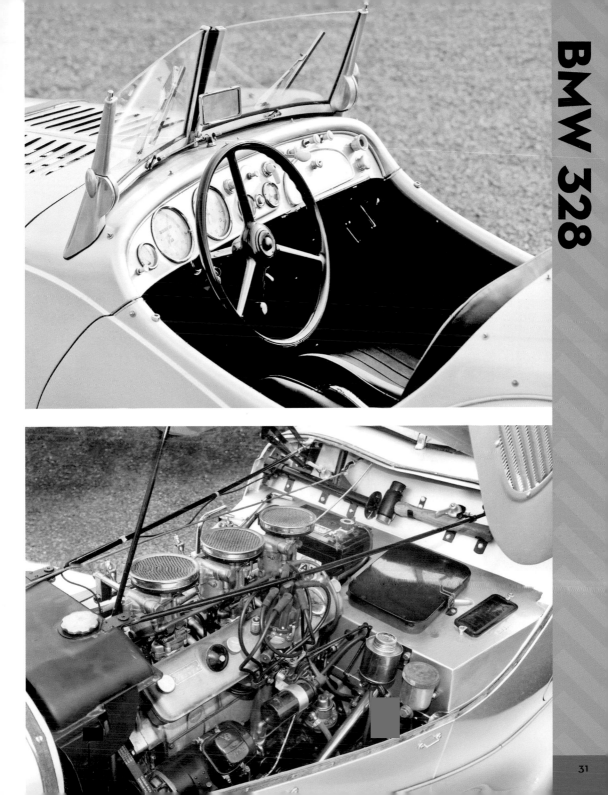

The Morgan Three-Wheeler is a cross between a car and a motorcycle; in some ways, it brings to mind a flightless World War I fighter plane. It has no doors and a low, cramped cockpit that sits so near to the ground that, when you are sitting in it, you can reach out and touch the road with your hand—although you'd risk burning that hand on the exhaust pipes running along the side.

The aircraft comparisons are apt on a number of levels. First produced in 1910, Morgan's Three-Wheeler got a new frame in 1933, but it was still a beautifully simple design

MORGAN THREE-WHEELER

Country of manufacture: U.K.
Year of production: 1909–1953
Engine: 990cc air-cooled Matchless overhead-valve V-twin
Output: 30 horsepower
Top speed: 80 miles per hour
Number built: approximately 30,000 (entire 44-year run)

with a tubular chassis, wood frame, and light aluminum panels. Power was transmitted from the air-cooled engine up front via a

propeller shaft to a chain-driven gearbox driving a single wheel at the back. That power was supplied by motorcycle engines, usually from JAP or Matchless. These powerplants were highly efficient in terms of power to weight and gave lively performance, although they were certainly a bit rough and noisy. The Supersports variant proved to have road-holding capabilities superior to most machines in its class and built a solid reputation in sprint and hillclimb events. Morgan advertised its machine as the "fastest three-wheeler in the world." Inexpensive to buy, maintain, and run, these cars have become the object of almost fanatical love for many enthusiasts.

Did You Know?

Morgan is the oldest surviving British carmaker. The company is based in Malvern and is still a family firm today, run by Charles Morgan, the grandson of founder H. F .S. Morgan. To celebrate the company's 100th anniversary in 2011, Morgan built a new three-wheeler that was shown at the 2011 Geneva Motor Show.

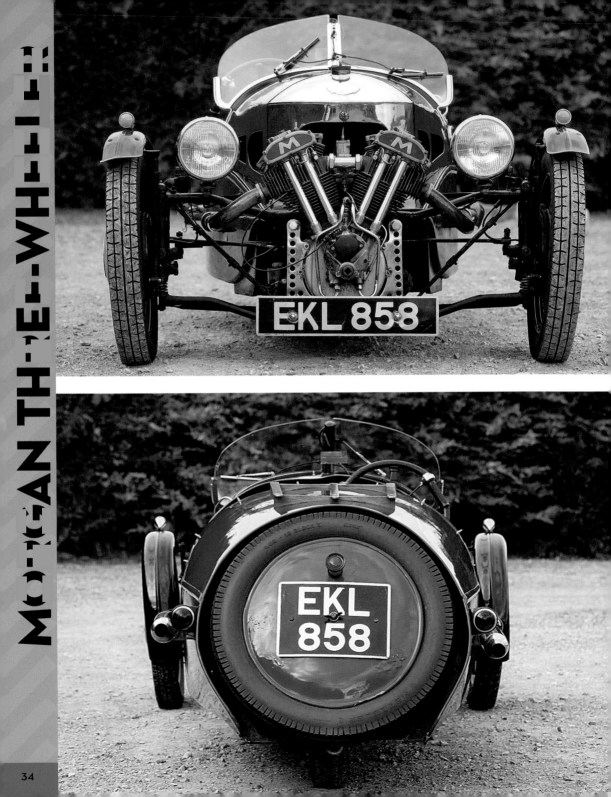

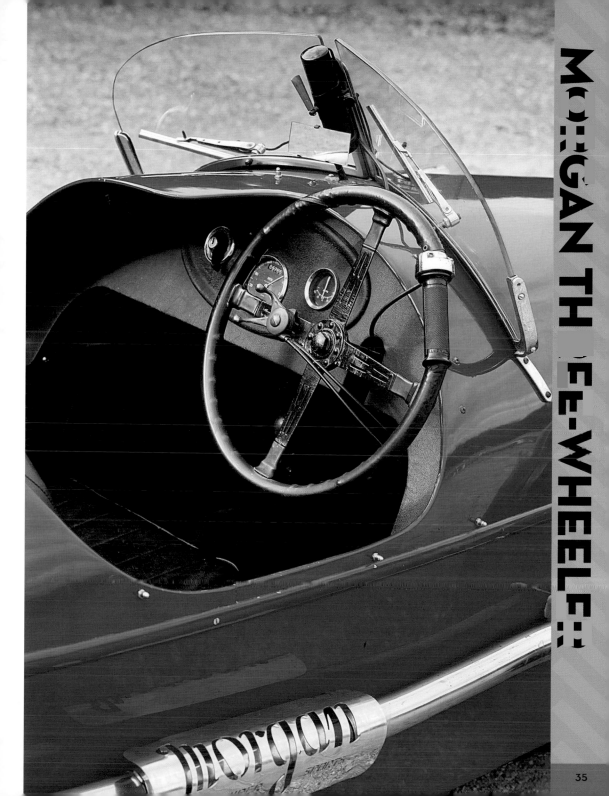

The fortunes of Sir Herbert Austin were closely tied to this humble little car, built in the Longbridge factory near Birmingham. The company was founded in 1905, and by 1939, when the Seven ceased production, nearly 300,000 of them had been built, with each model earning a £2 royalty for Austin himself. For the time, it was a considerable sum of money.

The Austin Seven was designed by Stanley Edge, a young draftsman in the drawing office, and Herbert Austin himself. Their goal was to counter the new horsepower-based taxes being enforced in the U.K. at the time. The lightweight 696cc four-cylinder engine was inspired by the FN motorcycle, with twin roller-bearing cranks splash-fed with oil. The car cost just £165

AUSTIN SEVEN

Country of manufacture: U.K.
Years of production: 1922–1939 (various iterations)
Engine: 696–747cc side-valve inline four-cylinder
Output: 7.2–33 horsepower
Top speed: 35–75 miles per hour (supercharged)
Number built: more than 290,000

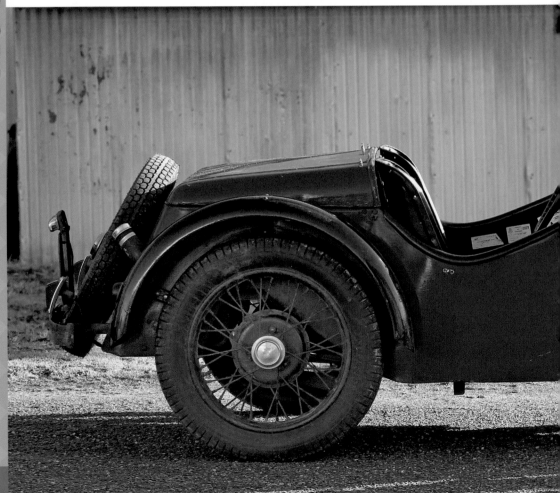

when new. Power was transmitted to the wheels through a three-speed gearbox, and brakes were in the form of cable-operated four-wheel brakes. On the early models, the front drums were operated by the handbrake. Output on those early cars was less than 10 horsepower, giving them a top speed of just 35 miles per hour.

Built in short- or long-wheelbase variants, with fabric or aluminum bodies mounted on an ash frame, the models had friendly names, such as the Ruby, Nippy, and Speedy. Although the factory did build a few sports versions, they numbered in the hundreds and were quite rare.

Most wannabe racers bought a cheap saloon, chopped or lifted off the body, and built a special for themselves.

The ultimate Sports Seven was the factory-built Ulster, with its A-frame chassis lowered and 5,000 rpm on tap. It was capable of over 70 miles per hour when supercharged. One of these cars finished third in the Ulster TT of 1929 driven by Archie Frazer Nash, just behind the 7.1-liter Mercedes of Rudolf Caracciola.

Did You Know?

Austin Sevens were made under license all over the world—Austin-licensed cars were called the Dixi in Germany, Rosengart in France, and Bantam in the United States. Colin Chapman, the man behind Lotus, based his first car on an Austin Seven.

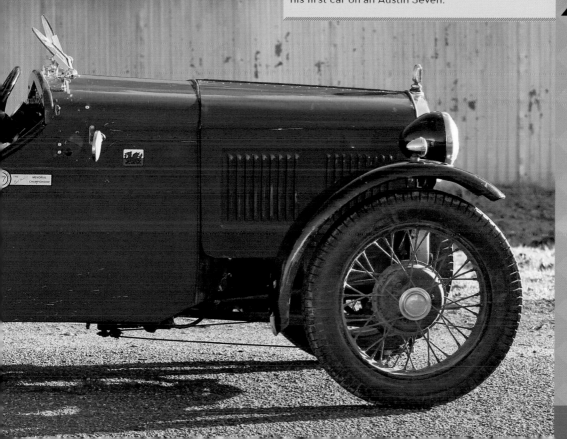

Considered by many to be the world's first sports car, the Jaguar SS100 made its debut at the London Motor Show in 1937. With a top speed over 100 miles per hour supplied by its new 3.5-liter inline-six engine, it could outperform virtually anything on the road. Great performance for under £450.

Sir William Lyons started out building very aerodynamic motorcycle sidecars. He progressed to producing automobiles at his Coventry works in 1931, under the name SS Cars. Despite being mocked by the purists of the day for their long showy wings, cut-away

doors, and folding windscreens, SS100s were the chosen transport for those who loved great speed and rakish looks at the right price.

JAGUAR SS100

Country of manufacture: U.K.
Years of production: 1936–1939
Engine: 2,663–3,485cc overhead-valve inline six-cylinder
Output: 125 horsepower
Top speed: 104 miles per hour
Number built: 314

Competition successes in the RAC, Monte Carlo, and Alpine rallies were matched on the track by race ace Tommy Wisdom, who set fastest lap in an SS100 at 118 miles per hour to win the autumn handicap at Brooklands in 1937. It was this race-prepped, stripped-down model that truly put Jaguar on the map.

The SS100 engine had started out in 1936 as a 2.5-liter, developed from the Standard unit. It was converted from side valve to overhead valve with a new cylinder head designed by engineers William Heynes and Harry Weslake. For 1937, it was enlarged to 3.5 liters, which delivered 125

horsepower through an excellent gearbox with synchromesh on three out of its four speeds.

When World War II erupted, SS100 production ceased, but Jaguar emerged from the conflict in fine fettle, building on its racing and engineering experience to produce a series of successful and popular sports cars.

Did You Know?

Harry Weslake, who designed the cylinder head for the SS100, would go on to design engines for Dan Gurney's famous Eagle-Weslake Formula 1 race car of the late 1960s.

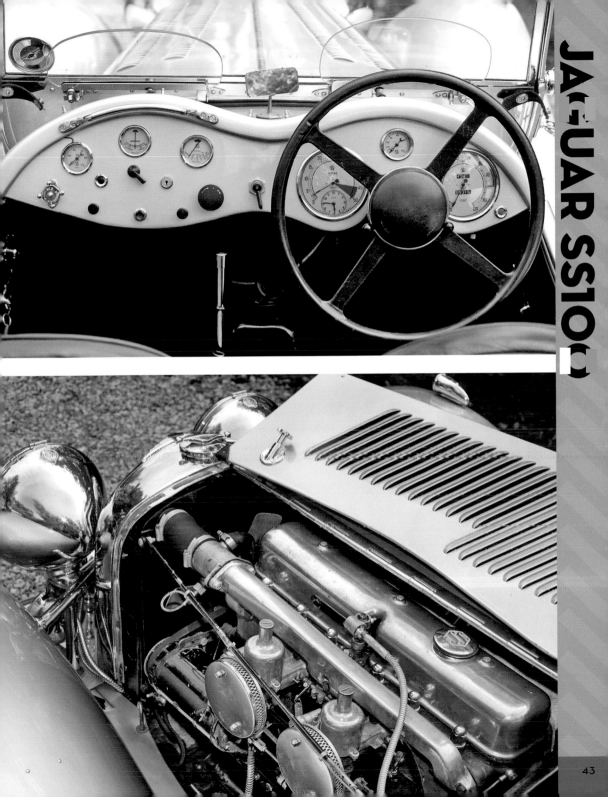

CHAPTER 2

THE 1950S: THE GOLDEN AGE

After World War II (1939–1945), European car manufacturing was in a terrible state. Automobile factories had spent the last decade producing war materiel, and the changeover back to building cars was slow and difficult.

For the first few years after the war, most of the "new" models produced were based on pre-1940 models. A few companies benefited from the stasis by relaunching earlier models with limited facelifts and equally limited investment. One of these companies was MG, which had been making quite a name for itself before the outbreak of the war. Its TB sports car had been released in 1939 and, with a little work, became the TC in 1945.

The TC was an immediate success. Many GIs bought them and took them home to the United States—the start of a special relationship that would endure for many years. Unlike anything available in the States, the MG TC was small, light, and nimble. The cars' simplicity was a virtue at that time; their early American owners had to be able to fix them when they broke because there was no dealer network yet in place.

Jaguar too was up and running quickly with its prewar saloons. In 1948, it created a sports car that was to set the benchmark for those to follow: the XK120. Porsche was likewise ahead of the game, and first prototypes of the 356 appeared the same year. Dr. Porsche and his team tackled the same lightweight engineering solutions in a different way.

By the early 1950s, the influx of European sports cars into the United States was being noticed by General Motors. With the rumor of a new Ford sports model on the drawing board, GM was galvanized into action. Sidestepping the need to build expensive and time-consuming metal tooling, in 1953 GM produced the first real American sports car, in the fiberglass-bodied Corvette, which would go on to become a legend.

In the early 1950s, Donald Healey recognized a gap in the U.S. sports car market; his stylish machine was created to fill a niche between the MG T series and the Jaguar XK120. In 1952, he introduced his fantastic new sports car to the world, and it was soon picked up by Len Lord at the British Motor Corporation, who renamed it the Austin-Healey 100. Bodies were built by Jensen in the Midlands with final assembly by MG at its Abingdon works. Healey's foresight would prove correct. Almost 80 percent of the cars ended up stateside. Initially equipped with a 2.6-liter four-cylinder engine, Healey introduced a six-cylinder version in 1956, along with a new, more aggressive body style. Three years later, the even-larger-capacity 3000 was put on sale.

Despite being hot, cramped, and extremely tail-happy in slippery conditions, the "Big Healeys" (as the six-cylinder versions were called) were and still are popular racing machines. They have competed in all the major sports car endurance events, including the Mille Miglia, 12 Hours of Sebring, and the 24 Hours of Le Mans—at times in the hands of

some of the greatest drivers of the day, including Stirling Moss and Carroll Shelby. BMC also had a highly successful works rally team with Timo Makkinen, Pat Moss, and Paddy Hopkirk achieving success in the Alpine and Monte Carlo rallies.

Evolving from Mks. I through III—eventually receiving front disc brakes, a wraparound windshield, a wooden dash, and wind-up windows—the Austin-Healey continued in production into 1968, to be replaced by BMC with the rather lackluster MG C.

AUSTIN-HEALEY 3000

Country of manufacture: U.K.
Years or production: 1959–1968
Engine: 2,912cc inline six-cylinder (3000 model)
Output: 124–150 horsepower
Top speed: 114–120 miles per hour
Number built: 42,926 (all models)

Did You Know?

In August 1956, Donald Healey drove a streamlined version of an Austin-Healey on the Bonneville Salt Flats in Utah, reaching a speed of 203.76 miles per hour.

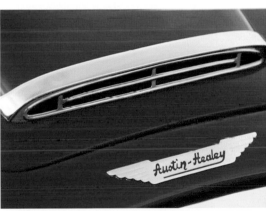

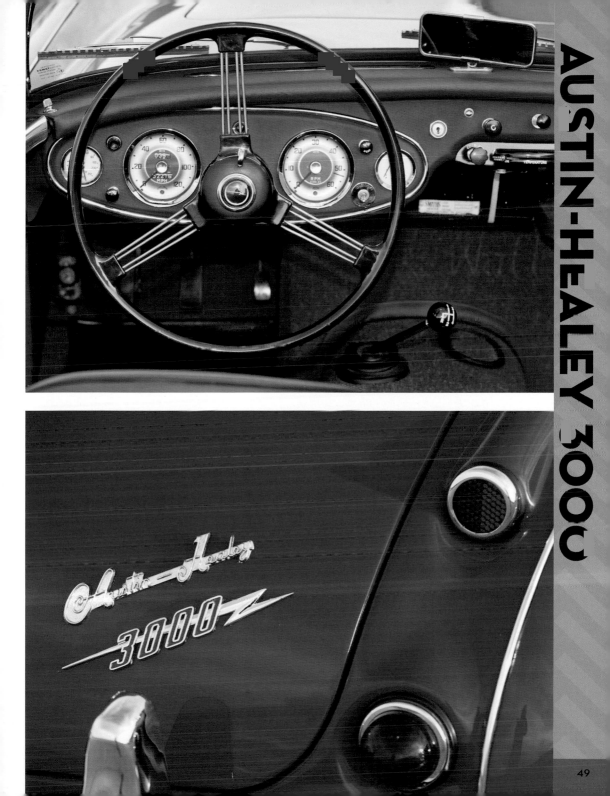

The MG T series had started back in 1936 with the TA, but many styling features date back even earlier to the M- and J-type Midgets.

After the war, MG was quick to capitalize on the emerging global market, basing the TC very much on its prewar cars. It had a traditional fold-flat windscreen, a flared arch and flowing steel body over an ash frame, with a nippy, straight four-cylinder overhead-valve engine. It cost just £547 on the home market in 1947.

The TC sold more units than MG had ever sold before, and in 1949 it was updated to the TD. The new model was available in left-hand drive for the U.S. market. It featured the better rack-and-pinion steering, bumpers, and independent front suspension. Coupled with

MG T SERIES

Country of manufacture: U.K.
Years of production: 1945–1955
Engine: 1,250–1,466cc overhead-valve inline four-cylinder
Output: 54–63 horsepower
Top speed: 86 miles per hour
Number built: 49,264

NO SMOKING
NO MATCHES
NO LIGHTS
ALLOWED

JE 8016

hydraulic brakes, the car was great fun and exciting to drive.

Special tuning kits were available from MG that could boost output to an impressive 90 horsepower, and TCs and TDs were popular budget racers. Many drivers started off their competition careers in one, including 1961 Formula 1 World Champion Phil Hill.

In 1953, a restyled TF model appeared. Effectively the same as the TD, it now had a sloping windscreen and lower bonnet line with faired-in headlamps and separate seats. It retained the 1,250cc motor. In its final year, the TF got the bigger 1,466cc engine, delivering a respectable 63 horsepower.

MG TCs and TDs sold so well in America that they opened up the U.S. market for the British sports cars invasion that was to come.

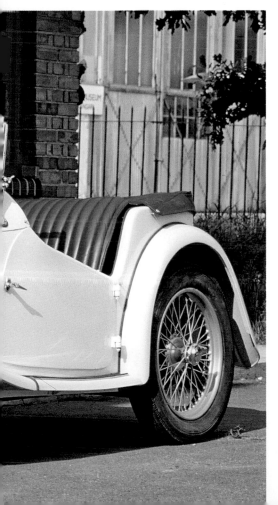

NO SMOKING
NO MATCHES
NO LIGHTS
ALLOWED

JE 8016

Sydney Allard had been highly successful before the war building fast Ford-based specials. After the war ended, he was quick off the mark with new cars. In 1952, he introduced the new-look K3, a car that would influence the sports car genre far beyond its brief production run. A very basic roadster, it was distinguished by the immensely powerful American V-8 engine under the hood—a Chrysler FirePower V-8 in the car shown here. The car sold mainly off the back of competition success after Allard himself won the Monte Carlo rally that year in an earlier model, narrowly beating Stirling Moss in his first rally.

ALLARD K3

Country of manufacture: U.K. (chassis)/United States (engine)
Years or production: 1952–1954
Engine: 3,622 or 4,375cc V-8 (Ford, Cadillac, or Chrysler)
Output: 180 horsepower
Top speed: 112 miles per hour
Number built: 62

The K3's fully enveloping steel body was stretched over a lightweight tubular frame with twin fuel tanks in the rear. A wide

cockpit allowed seating for three abreast, with a floor-mounted side gear shift into a three-speed gearbox. The roadster had an unusually generous amount of space in the back for luggage. Motors were either from Ford (mostly for the U.K. market), Cadillac, or Chrysler FirePower "Hemis" (usually for the U.S. market). Suspension was semi-independent swing axle with coil springs on the front, and a de Dion tube at the rear; brakes were hydraulically operated drums all round.

The cars were raced extensively in the United States due to their excellent power-to-weight ratio. Drivers who competed in Allards included Carroll Shelby and Zora Arkus-Duntov—who raced a K3 at Le Mans. A few years later, each of these men would be pivotal figures in bringing the successful Allard formula of an American V-8 engine in a light chassis to even greater heights through the AC Shelby Cobra and Chevrolet Corvette.

Did You Know?

Sydney Allard is considered to be the father of British drag racing. In 1961, he built an incredible supercharged Chrysler-powered slingshot dragster with which he recorded a 10.48-second quarter-mile run, the fastest mile recorded in the U.K. at that time. In 1991, Sydney Allard was inducted into the International Drag Racing Hall of Fame.

The "Frogeye"—or "Bugeye," as it was nicknamed in the United States—was designed by Healey's Gerry Coker and made under license by BMC at the MG works in Abingdon. It was built to be a successor to the sport versions of the Austin Seven, i.e., inexpensive to buy and run. It featured the great little A-series straight-four engine as seen in the Austin A35, but with twin SU carburetors and a tuned engine under the one-piece bonnet. It also had the very quick, precise rack-and-pinion steering from the Morris Minor and a short, sporty gear lever.

The signature headlamps sticking out of the bonnet were originally designed to flip over, but the mechanicals proved too expensive, so they were left fixed, giving the car its cutesy character. The early Sprite sold well, particularly to women, but it was not particularly practical,

with trunk access only from behind the seats. And if you wanted to turn on the heater, you had to stop and open the hood to do so. Yet the Frogeye sold for just £660, almost half the price of most other sports cars on the market at the time. Surprisingly, the cars were a hit with a number of racers, as they were easy to tune and predictable on the track. Stirling Moss and his sister Pat both raced them.

AUSTIN-HEALEY "FROGEYE" SPRITE

Country of manufacture: U.K.
Years of production: 1958–1961
Engine: 948cc
Output: 43 horsepower
Top speed: 82.9 miles per hour
Number built: 48,987

Did You Know?

In 1959, three Sprites were entered into the famous 12-hour race held in Sebring, Florida. Modified by the BMC competition department with bigger 1 1/4 twin SU carburetors and four-wheel disc brakes, they finished first, second, and third in class, giving the little car valuable publicity in the important U.S. market.

PTK 269

The MGA's stunning, slippery shape was a radical departure from the boxy profile of the prewar T series. It came from a prototype built by MG's brilliant designer, Sydney Enever, around an MG TD chassis that ran (rather unsuccessfully) at Le Mans in 1952. However, the MGA was not put into production at the time because Len Lord, the BMC chairman, had signed a deal with Donald Healey to produce Austin-Healeys and didn't want to create his own competition. After a three-year

MGA

Country of manufacture: U.K.
Years of production: 1955–1958
Engine: 1,489cc–1,622cc inline four-cylinder
Output: 68–85 horsepower
Top speed: 95 miles per hour
Number built: 101,587

wait, the MGA finally made its debut at the Frankfurt Auto Show. MG chose to name it the "A" because it was "the first of a new line."

The MGA was the first modern sporting MG, with twin SU carburetors, the great BMC B-series engine, and 72 horsepower on tap. Under the skin lay a robust box-section chassis and conventional suspension with many of its parts standard Austin or Morris components, which helped to keep the price low. Built mainly for the U.S. market, at £844 it was cheaper than the Triumph TR3 and Austin-Healey 100, and MG sold over 13,000 units in the car's first year.

A coupe appeared in 1956; its superior aerodynamics made it a bit faster, and an even quicker twin-cam model followed in 1958. The latter was the first production car to feature all-around disc brakes, making the MGA probably the first car in the MG line to really live up to the "Safety Fast" motto.

Did You Know?
Of the 101,587 MGAs built, 80 percent were sold in the United States.

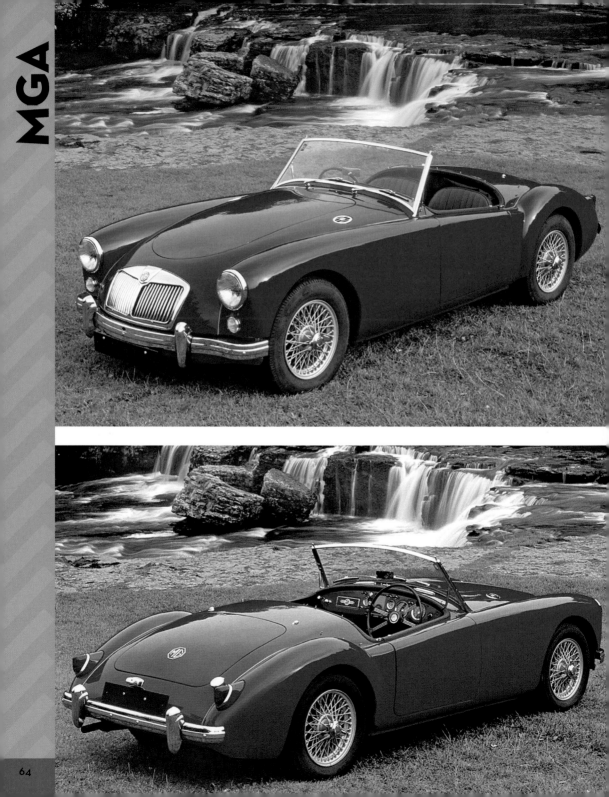

Launched at the London Motor Show in 1948, the XK120 was originally created for a limited production run to stimulate interest in Jaguar after the war years and to sell the company's saloon models. But show visitors were bowled over by the sweeping lines and promised performance of the new William Lyons–designed car. Starved of motoring excitement since before the war, sporting drivers sent orders rolling in, and Jaguar happily changed its plans. The first 242 cars were hand-built with aluminum panels over ash frames until tooling was completed to make more economical pressed-steel bodies. Even then, the hood, trunk, and door panels remained aluminum.

The fabulous dual-overhead-cam straight-six engine was Jaguar's own design. It was not only strong—with seven main bearings—but also powerful, delivering 160 horsepower, enough to propel the lightweight car to over 120 miles per hour. The top speed was respectable enough that Jaguar incorporated it into the XK's name. Competition success followed with a 1–2–3

finish at Silverstone in 1949. Later that year, Ian Appleyard famously won the Alpine rally in an XK120.

A stunning coupe arrived in 1951, followed by a more luxurious drop-head coupe in 1953. The XK120's gearbox was a four-speed manual with synchromesh on the top three speeds. Suspension was independent at the front with wishbones and torsion bars, and a live rear axle and semi-elliptical springs for the rear. The Jaguar used hydraulically operated drum brakes all around.

JAGUAR XK120

Country of manufacture: U.K.
Years of production: 1948–1954
Engine: 3,442cc DOHC inline six-cylinder
Output: 160 horsepower
Top speed: 120 miles per hour
Number built: 12,078

Did You Know?

In May 1949, the XK120 was speed tested on the long Jabbeke straight in Belgium. With windshield removed, the sleek cat achieved a speed of 136.59 miles per hour, making it the fastest production car in the world at the time.

Designed by legendary GM stylist Harley Earl in response to the flood of European sports cars making their way into the United States, the Corvette was the first true American sports car. It was also the world's first mass-production car built using a glass-fiber body shell.

Revealed at the GM Motorama in January 1953, Chevrolet built only 300 cars that year, and the hand-built design caused Chevrolet to lose money on each of them, casting doubts over the car's future. It was the imminent appearance of Ford's new Thunderbird model that spurred GM executives to push ahead with the Corvette.

The early models were more show than go, featuring Chevrolet's Blue Flame 235-cubic-inch straight-six motor in the 1953 cars, a motor that was upgraded to a more powerful

150-horsepower version in the 1954 cars. The first-series Corvettes were available only as roadsters; the cockpit was cramped and the dash layout impractical, with most of the dials in the center of the console. The original Corvettes had solid axle springs, with independent rear suspension not appearing until the second-generation Sting Ray models beginning in 1963.

Chevrolet would continue to make annual improvements to its fledgling sports car throughout the 1950s. The car's third year, 1955, saw the introduction of a more robust 265-cubic-inch V-8 motor, and in 1956 a new body arrived with scalloped sides and a fresh front. The Corvette was beginning to evolve into something truly special. By this time, Zora Arkus-Duntov had arrived at Chevrolet and would have a big influence on the Corvette; for 1957 he matched up a four-speed manual transmission with the new 283-cubic-inch V-8, bringing another performance upgrade. By the end of the Corvette's first-generation run, the familiar Chevy small-block engine would eventually reach 327 cubic inches. But even greater things were to come the following year. Note: the turquoise car shown is a 1957 model; the red model is a 1961; the black is a 1954.

CHEVROLET CORVETTE (FIRST GENERATION)

Country of manufacture: United States
Years of production: 1953–1962
Engine: varies
Output: 150–340 horsepower
Top speed: 107 miles per hour
Number built: 69,015 (all model years, 1953–1962)

Did You Know?

Chevrolet public relations department employee Myron Scott is credited for suggesting the Corvette name, which he found in a dictionary. A corvette is a small, maneuverable warship.

By no means a replica, the Morgan is the real thing: a car of 1930s lineage that you can still buy today. Hand-crafted in Malvern by the same family-owned company for over 100 years, the Morgan's flowing steel wings are stretched over ash frames, making the body both light and easy to repair.

The Plus 4 was first introduced in 1950 as a follow-on from the successful 4/4 prewar model. With a flat radiator grille, it was initially equipped with a 70-horsepower Standard Vanguard 2-liter engine. This powerplant was soon upgraded to the TR2 unit, with 90

MORGAN PLUS 4

Country of manufacture: U.K.
Years of production: 1950–present
Engine: 1,991cc Rover DOHC inline four (shown)
Output: 95–145 braking horsepower
Top speed: 120 miles per hour
Number built: 4,584

horsepower. Power kept going up, from 95 to 105 horsepower with the TR3 motor in 1961, to 125 horses with the Lawrence-tuned Super Sport models of the 1960s. The chassis

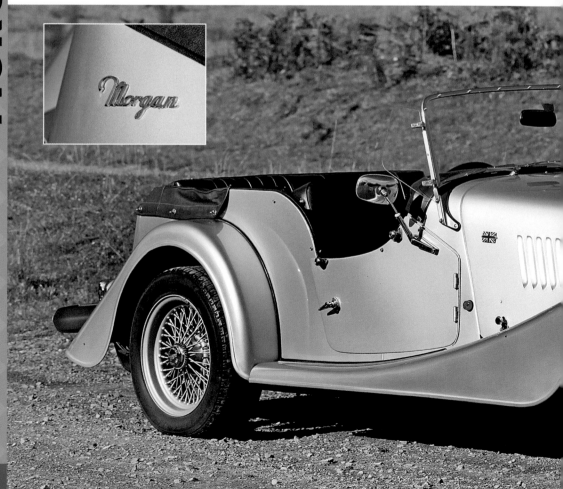

was a simple steel ladder frame with Morgan's famous and still-surviving sliding-pillar front suspension, with live axle and leaf springs at the back. Bodies, available in two- or four-seat sports or drop-head coupes, now had their distinctive waterfall grille.

Starting out with hydraulically operated drum brakes, the Plus 4 got discs in 1960. A special low-line body for competition was available with alloy panels from 1966 onward. A Morgan Plus 4 won its class at Le Mans in 1962 with ace tuner Chris Lawrence behind the wheel. Production stopped and started over the years and was last revived in 2005 with the 145-horsepower Ford Duratec 16-valve powerplant. The car shown here was manufactured in 1994 and has the excellent Rover DOHC 16-valve Tomcat engine.

Did You Know?

The 1964 Plus 4 Plus was an ill-conceived fiberglass-bodied coupe. Looking like a stretched Lotus Elite, it went down like a lead balloon with Morgan's conservative clientele and only 50 units were sold.

M379 XST

Looking to gain a foothold in the lucrative U.S. market, BMW asked German aristocrat Albrecht Goetz—who ran a U.S.-based industrial design agency—to come up with a new sports car similar to the Mercedes 300SL. Goetz consulted with influential U.S. importer Max Hoffman and came up with the very handsome 507 that was unveiled at the 1955 Frankfurt Auto Show. Using a shortened chassis from the 503, the 507 sported an all-aluminum high-compression V-8 engine matched to a four-speed gearbox. Its body was finished in alloy panels.

The 507 featured many innovations, including an internally adjustable wing mirror and an adjustable steering column; early cars were fitted with drum brakes, but later models received discs and an optional hardtop to finish off the racy, elegant profile. The car even had an internal safety frame to protect the driver in the event of an accident.

Despite its beauty, the 507 never sold in the numbers BMW had hoped for. At almost $9,000, the hand-built model cost nearly three times more than a Corvette. BMW managed only a short production run of 253 cars—instead of the 5,000 Hoffman had predicted—and the entire episode nearly bankrupted the company. However, these hardships didn't stop the manufacturer from borrowing 507 styling cues for its Z8 decades later.

BMW 507

Country of manufacture: Germany
Years of production: 1955–1957
Engine: 3,168cc aluminum V-8
Output: 150 horsepower
Top speed: 135 miles per hour
Number built: 253

Did You Know?

Albrecht Goetz's most famous design would appear at the end of the following decade, in the form of the Datsun 240Z.

Initially, Enzo Ferrari saw making road cars merely as a means to finance his racing endeavors, but he soon realized there was a growing market for *gran turismo* (GT) models and began to direct more effort and resources into this potentially lucrative field.

The first 250GT was unveiled at the Paris Motor Show in 1954, following the lackluster 250 Europa of the previous year. The GT's 3-liter V-12 engine, designed by Gioacchino Colombo, had started out as a racing engine at just 1.5 liters. It was light, high-revving, and strong, with a five main-bearing bottom end. The chassis was a tubular steel space

FERRARI 250GT

Country of manufacture: Italy
Years of production: 1956–1964
Engine: 2,935cc DOHC V-12
Output: 240 horsepower
Top speed: 140 miles per hour
Number built: 2,500 (all models)

frame sporting numerous body styles, mostly designed by Pininfarina. These variants included a 2+2 coupe, cabriolet, short-wheelbase (SWB) Berlinetta, California, Lusso, and the highly prized GTO. In competition,

the 250GTs were lightened with alloy panels and their power was boosted to nearly 300 horsepower in the short wheelbase.

The full sports racer 250 Testarossa won the world sports car championship in 1958, 1960, and 1961, and featured six Weber carburetors rather than the usual three in the GT. Drum brakes were replaced with discs and, when this setup was transferred to the SWB chassis by Giotto Bizzarrini, the 250GTO was born.

In 1962, reigning Formula 1 World Champion Phil Hill raced a 250GTO to a superb second place in the 12-hour race at Sebring. The GTO went on to win the GT championship in 1962, 1963, and 1964. The car shown here is a 1957 250GT cabriolet with a body by Pininfarina. Only 36 were built, no two of which are identical.

Did You Know?

The name 250 came from the capacity of a single cylinder in cubic centimeters, following Ferrari's early nomenclature. GTO comes from the Italian, *gran turismo omologato*, meaning a grand-touring car built in adequate numbers to qualify as a production-based race car. Ferrari was supposed to build 100 GTOs according to the Fédération Internationale de l'Automobile's (FIA) GT homologation rules but in fact made only 39, duping the sanctioning body by leaving large gaps in the chassis numbers of the cars.

When the Porsche 356 first appeared in 1948, it was essentially a fast Volkswagen with streamlined bodywork. Through numerous technical developments and engine upgrades, the car moved progressively away from its origins. By the time the 356B was introduced in 1959, there were almost no VW parts left in the model.

Ferry Porsche, son of Dr. Ferdinand, was responsible for the 356, the first car to be badged Porsche. Its body shape was penned by Austrian Irwin Kommeda. Throughout its 16-year run, the car used an air-cooled, horizontally opposed, four-cylinder engine

PORSCHE 356

Country of manufacture: Germany
Years of production: 1948–1965
Engine: Air-cooled 1,100–1,966cc overhead-valve four cylinder
Output: 130 horsepower
Top speed: 130 miles per hour
Number built: 82,363

mounted behind the rear axle. Output increased from just 40 horsepower in the first 1,086cc engine right up to 130 horsepower in the final 1964 2.0-liter incarnation. With

a complex independent suspension system ironing out its tail-happy balance problems, the lightweight 356 handled well, although full attention was needed in fast corners.

The cars were an instant hit, and the little Porsche's reputation climbed rapidly on the track, with class wins at Le Mans and the Mille Miglia, and associations with movie stars such as Steve McQueen and James Dean, who owned them.

For 1955, the Carrera arrived for advanced students only. No longer a pushrod engine, the Carrera mill used four overhead cams, dry sump, and a roller bearing main for strength. It was good for over 120 miles per hour in tuned 1.5-liter form. Porsche also offered a whole range of body styles, including convertibles, coupes, and a Speedster model with a low windscreen and Spartan interior.

Did You Know?
The Porsche badge was designed in 1952 on Dr. Ferry Porsche's napkin as he sat opposite U.S. importer Max Hoffman in a New York restaurant.

Seeing the success of Jaguar's XK120 in America, Triumph badly wanted a slice of the sports car export market. After a bid to take over Morgan was rejected, Triumph lashed together a car for the 1952 London Motor Show. Called the TS20, it was ugly, ill-conceived, and overshadowed by the launch of the stunning Austin-Healey 100 at the same event.

A year later, Triumph returned, this time offering the much-admired TR2, with cutaway doors and a distinctive pinched-waist shape. It featured a tuned version of the old Vanguard 2-liter engine and a ladder chassis designed by

TRIUMPH TR2/3/3A
Country of manufacture: U.K.
Years of production: 1953–1962
 (TR2 through TR3B)
Engine: 1,991–2,138cc
Output: 90–100 horsepower
Top speed: 103–110 miles per hour
Number built: 80,241

Ken Richardson. With coil-spring suspension and wishbones at the front, and a live rear axle on semi-elliptical springs at the back, the car

was predictable in corners and easy to correct if things got out of hand.

The TR2 (the dark green car below) became a legend in its own lifetime, competing in the Mille Miglia and at Le Mans, and building a large fan base of loyal owners who loved the short little car's sparky performance and great handling. Such widespread support made it Triumph's top dollar earner.

In 1953, the TR3 arrived with a new grille and a bit more power; this was the first mass-produced car that featured disc brakes as standard. The TR3A (the red car next page) arrived in 1957 and sold better than ever, with over 50,000 units leaving the Coventry factory. This facelift included external door handles along with slightly recessed headlamps. In its final incarnation, sometimes called the TR3B, the roadster received a bigger engine and the new, all synchromesh TR4 gearbox.

Did You Know?

The company went bankrupt before the war, and Triumph's name was bought by Standard in 1944. The TR2 features the badges of both companies, Standard on the nose and Triumph on the hubcaps.

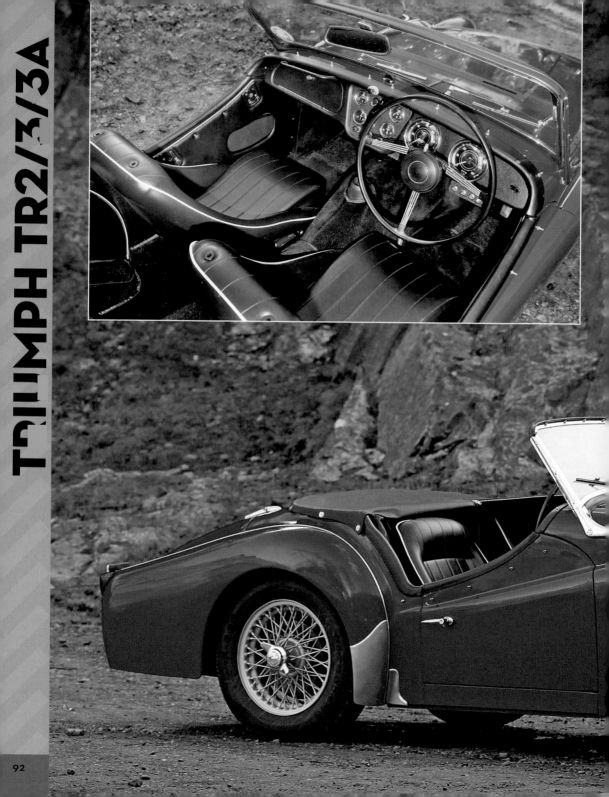

CHAPTER 3
CLASSIC SPORTS CARS OF THE 1960s

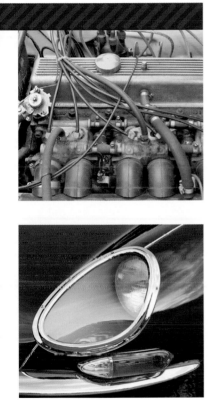

As the hardships and tough commercial environment of the 1950s faded in Europe, economies expanded quickly. People had more money in their pockets; an age of optimism had arrived. Customers wanted a bit more than the Spartan cockpits and harsh handling of the early sports cars, and the manufacturers delivered. Italian and British manufacturers were ready with designs for faster, more exciting cars. The GT era was born.

Aston Martin launched the DB5, gaining great notoriety and sales when the car appeared in the James Bond movies. Jaguar, building on the competition success of its C-type and D-type sports racers, delivered the E-type—a stunning blend of artistry and performance that would achieve iconic status by the end of its run in 1974. MG produced its ubiquitous and affordable B, selling more than half a million units, while at the other end of the scale, AC was dragged from near obscurity by a tall Texan who thought a lightweight British roadster could be a monster on road and track with a potent V-8 under its hood.

In Italy, Ferrari introduced its 275-range of V-12 quad-cam sports cars in 1964, with lines penned by the now-indispensable Pininfarina. Toward the end of the decade, Enzo dabbled with badge engineering, creating the Dino based on a design by his son of the same name.

In the United States, General Motors had gotten over its cold feet with the Corvette and produced its most revered model, the Sting Ray. Available as a coupe for the first time, the Corvette featured such innovative engineering as pop-up headlights, independent suspension, and fuel injection, and it was touted by the press as "tomorrow's car today!"

JAGUAR E-TYPE (XKE)

Unveiled in 1961 to great fanfare—Enzo Ferrari himself is reported to have said that the new car was "the most beautiful car ever made"—the Jaguar E-type is one of the world's most legendary sports cars. Its stunning shape came from the pen of aerodynamicist Malcolm Sayer, who was given free rein to design the most streamlined monocoque body the wind tunnel could deliver. When it first went on sale, Jaguar struggled to keep up with demand.

Under its long hood was the 13-year-old XK6 engine bored out to 3.8 liters. While well-proven in the C- and D-types, the motor had become a bit dated, and it was replaced by the better 4.2-liter version in October 1964. Independent rear suspension with coil springs and a torsion

JAGUAR E-TYPE (XKE)
Country of manufacture: U.K.
Years of production: 1961–1975
Engine: 3,781–4,235cc DOHC inline six-cylinder or 5,343cc DOHC V-12
Output: 220 horsepower (six-cylinder), 272 horsepower (V-12)
Top speed: 150 miles per hour
Number built: 72,520

bar on the front end, coupled with a low ground clearance of just 5 inches, made for great handling. Although steering lacked precision in the earlier iterations, Jaguar soon addressed the problem with a rack-and-pinion system. There were also all-around disc brakes as standard now, in inboard configuration at the rear.

A whole range of models (named XKE for the U.S. market) arrived, including a 2+2, coupes, and in 1971, a brand-new 5.3-liter V-12 series III—the first volume production V-12 since Lincoln's in 1948. While it lacked some of the subtleties of the first cars, the new beefed-up E-type, sporting wide arches and big tires, was a hit all over again, and included power steering, ventilated disc brakes, and an early form of Lucas-Opus electronic ignition. The last special-edition E-types, 50 in number, rolled off the production line in Coventry in 1974, the end of a great milestone in sports car history.

Did You Know?

In 1960, American team owner and long-time Jaguar privateer racer Briggs Cunningham entered the very first E-type prototype mule in the 24 Hours of Le Mans. The car was painted in Cunningham's famous blue-and-white color scheme, and at the wheel were two legendary American racers, Dan Gurney and Walt Hansgen. That car, code-named E2A, still survives today.

The new TR4 was designed by Italian stylist Giovanni Michelotti with a full-width pressed steel body, bonnet power bulge for the carburetors, a bigger trunk, wind-up windows, and the first fascia-mounted adjustable ventilation.

Under the skin was the same strong and torquey 2.2-liter four-cylinder engine seen in earlier TRs, although the twin SU carburetors were replaced in late 1962 with Strombergs. There was synchromesh on all forward gears, and an optional electrically operated overdrive now gave seven speeds in a close-ratio gearbox. Steering was rack and pinion, featuring one of the first collapsible columns. The TR4's detachable Surrey top was a useful innovation, allowing removal of the roof panel alone with the fixed rear window staying in place. Porsche would use this system later in its Targa models.

In 1963, California engineer Kas Kastner entered three cars in the Sebring 12-hour race, finishing a respectable first, second, and fourth in class. In 1965, the TR4A was launched, sporting a new grille and independent rear suspension, replacing the now-antiquated TR2 setup carried through to previous TRs. The new suspension added weight, however, and slowed performance, causing critics to say that the TR4A didn't handle as well as the previous car.

TRIUMPH TR4/4A

Country of manufacture: U.K.
Years of production: 1961–1967
Engine: 1,991cc–2,138cc overhead-valve inline four-cylinder
Output: 105 horsepower
Top speed: 110 miles per hour
Number built: 68,718

Did You Know?

In 1962, a limited run of bespoke coupes, designed and built by Harrington, was made for London dealer Dove. Called the Dove GTR4, only 55 were eventually ordered, as they cost the same as a new E-type.

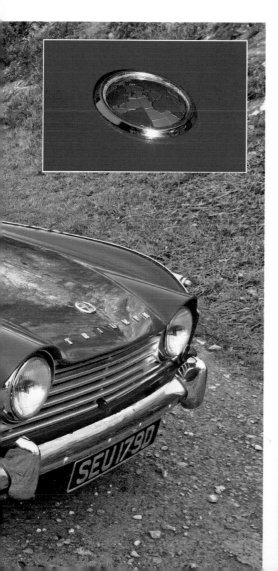

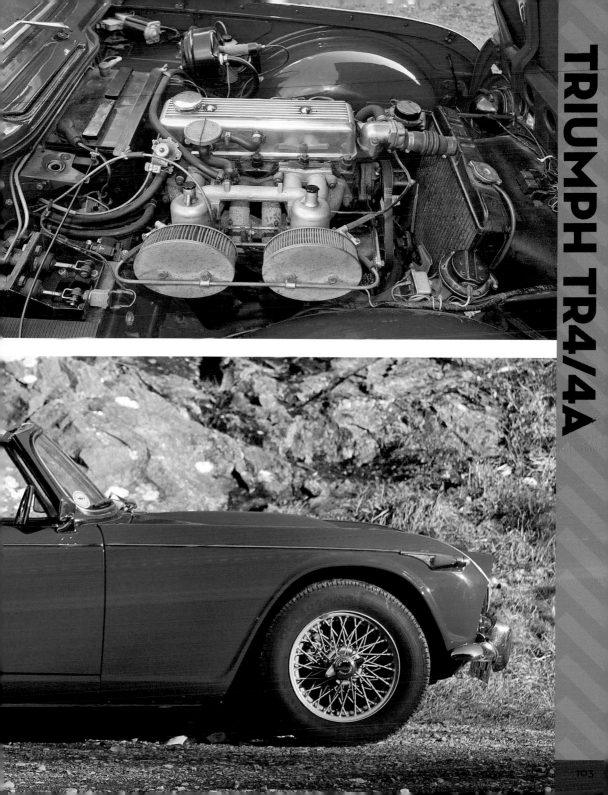

When one-time Texan chicken farmer Carroll Shelby first raced a Cadillac V-8-powered Allard J2 in 1952, he was turned on to the fact that the marriage of a lightweight British chassis to American power really worked. After a short but successful racing career—which included winning Le Mans in a works Aston Martin in 1959—Shelby was forced to give up driving race cars. Instead, he turned his considerable intellect and energy to building them, with an eye toward to taking on the Ferraris, who were unbeatable at the time.

Not wanting to start from scratch, and recalling his earlier experiences racing the Allard, he looked around for a sports car into which he could shoehorn Ford's powerful new V-8 engine. After Austin-Healey showed little interest, Shelby found a partner with the pretty but antiquated John Tojeiro–designed Barchetta, the AC Ace.

The Ace was an ideal platform, featuring alloy panels stretched over a lightweight tubular frame. In the first of his Anglo-American hybrids, Shelby fitted Ford's 260-cubic-inch V-8

into the engine bay, followed shortly thereafter by the 289, which offered startling performance including a 0 to 60 time of just 5.5 seconds. With outboard disc brakes all around and rack-and-pinion steering, the cars were immediately successful on the track, racing at Daytona, Sebring, and Watkins Glen.

In 1964, Shelby wanted to compete in Europe, but he knew that the open-top roadster would never have the aerodynamic efficiency to keep up on the long straights of Le Mans and the Nürburgring. So he got designer Peter Brock to build a coupe body, and the Cobra Daytona was born. Winning the world GT championship in 1965, it remains the only American car ever to achieve this feat.

The Cobra's final incarnation housed Ford's race-bred 427-cubic-inch side-oiler V-8 and was the world's fastest-accelerating production car in 1967. Bearing fat arches front and rear, it bore only a passing resemblance to the 289 version, sharing only its doors and bonnet.

AC COBRA

Country of manufacture: UK (chassis)/United States (engine)
Years of production: 1962–1968
Engine: 260-, 289-, or 427-cubic-inch Ford V-8
Output: 425 horsepower (427-cubic-inch engine)
Top speed: 138 miles per hour (289-cubic-inch version); 165 miles per hour (427); 195 miles per hour (Cobra Daytona coupe)
Number built: 996 (all versions)

Did You Know?

In 1966, the race rules were changed and the six Daytona Cobra coupes were shipped back from Europe to the United States, where Shelby struggled to sell them. Had you picked one up at the time, you could sell it today for about $10 million!

Before the Giulietta, Alfa Romeo was more associated with racing cars than road-going vehicles, but the new car propelled the company into big-time mass production. The Giulia Spider was an updated version of the Giulietta Spider first launched in 1955. The new model now featured Alfa's fabulous, free-revving, 1,570cc chain-driven twin-cam engine—with dual carburetors for the Veloce-tuned option. Suspension was still by way of independent coil springs on the front and trailing arm, with coil springs on the back mounted on a rigid axle.

The beautiful monocoque bodywork by Pininfarina came at a cost. When first released, this little car was priced higher than a Jaguar

XK150, yet it was so glamorous that every starlet wanted to be seen in one. The Giulia set new standards of refinement with its roomy cabin and elegant cockpit layout, and the excellent engine gave performance to match. A column-shifted five-speed gearbox gave it long legs for freeway driving. The car featured disc brakes on the front on later models.

ALFA ROMEO GIULIA SPIDER

Country of manufacture: Italy
Years of production: 1962–1965
Engine: 1,570cc double overhead-valve inline four-cylinder
Output: 112 horsepower
Top speed: 106 miles per hour
Number built: 10,341

Did You Know?

The Pininfarina car design and coachbuilding firm was founded as Carrozzeria Pinin Farina in 1930 by Battista "Pinin" Farina. His nickname referred to his being the youngest brother in his family. The company would eventually change its name to today's Pininfarina and Farina himself had his official name changed to Pininfarina in 1961.

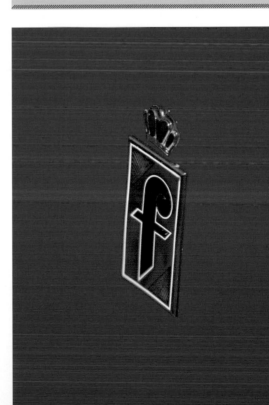

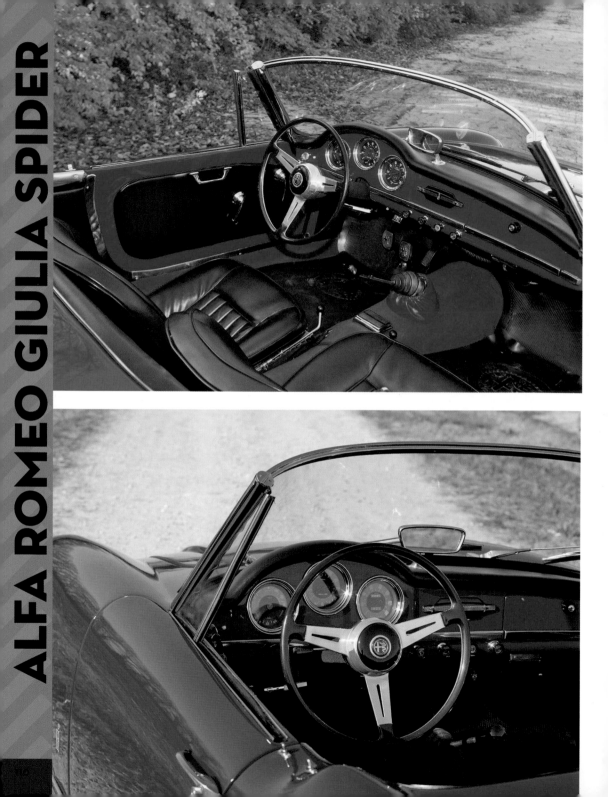

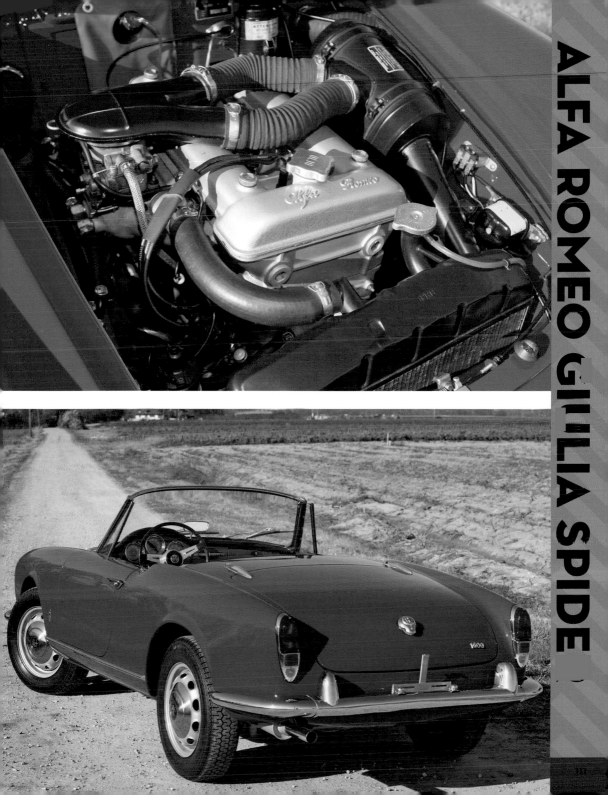

Colin Chapman got his start tuning Austin Sevens and building trials cars in a London garage in 1952. Just 10 years later, when the first Lotus Elan came out, he had already tasted success with a series of Lotus Sevens and the much-admired Elite.

The Elan was built around a Y-shaped pressed-and-welded steel chassis that had initially been designed as a temporary structure to hang the body from during development. However, it was strong and simple, so it stuck. The one-piece fiberglass body was light and easy

LOTUS ELAN SPRINT

Country of manufacture: U.K.
Years of production: 1962–1973
Engine: 1,558cc DOHC straight four
Output: 126 horsepower (Sprint)
Top speed: 120 miles per hour
Number built: 12,200

to build but had no structural rigidity—unlike its monocoque predecessor, the Elite.

Under the bonnet, a Ford Cortina 1,500cc block was mated to the wonderful twin-cam

cross-flow cylinder head and supplied with plenty of fuel by twin Weber carburetors. Combined with a big-valve head, the last Elan Sprint delivered more than 120 horsepower and accelerated from 0 to 60 miles per hour in an impressive 6.7 seconds—quicker than the Lamborghini Islero. The Elan Sprint could also reach up to 80 miles per hour faster than a Porsche 911E or even a Ferrari Dino. This great handling little sports car was a total innovation, much loved by back-road racers and motor-club eventers.

The Elan's comfort and agility were partly due to the Chapman struts—combined springs and dampers mounted on chassis outriggers, which made up the all-around independent suspension. With disc brakes on each wheel, it was quite a package, and cheap, too. The Elan was even available as a home-build kit.

Did You Know?

The Elan was one of the truly glamorous British cars of the age. Fans of the classic 1960s British television show *The Avengers* will recall occasionally seeing an Elan driven by the program's equally alluring leading lady, Mrs. Emma Peel (played by Diana Rigg). When movie legend Peter Sellers married actress Britt Ekland, he gave her a Lotus Elan as a gift.

MG's follow-up to its shapely A arrived in 1962. It was considerably more advanced, being of monocoque construction with a bigger, B series engine. Although marginally shorter, it offered more room in the cockpit. The investment that went into tooling up for the MGB meant the car had to be a big seller for the company to recoup its costs. After some initial problems with body rigidity, MG got the B in order. It proved to be a reliable, practical sports car that sold like hotcakes, particularly in the United States.

MGB

Country of manufacture: U.K.
Years of production: 1962–1980
Engine: 1,798cc overhead valve inline four
Output: 95 horsepower
Top speed: 105 miles per hour
Number built: 534,352

For maximum sales, MG strategically chose to draw as broadly from the marketplace as possible, and the B was one of the first sports cars to be marketed to both sexes, with

brochures showing women enjoying their MGBs at the beach, on the freeway, etc. Nearly 500,000 rolled out of the Abingdon factory over the model's long production history, including a GT version in 1965 with a tin top, two small seats in the back, and one of the first tailgates.

In 1974, the U.S. government tightened its emissions standards, forcing MG to de-tune the cars with a single Stromberg carburetor in place of the twin SUs. Further ignominy followed when the headlights were deemed too low for new federal regulations. MG's fix was to raise the ride height, causing a predictable reduction in handling responsiveness. Finally, in 1980, when the B was long past its sell-by date and unable to compete with more modern cars, MG scrapped the model and the storied Abingdon plant closed—the end of an era for sports cars and for the British motor industry.

Did You Know?

In 1992, a derivative of the B with Rover V-8 power surfaced as the MGRV8, a luxurious but bloated caricature of the old car; of the 2,000 produced, more than 1,500 went to Japan.

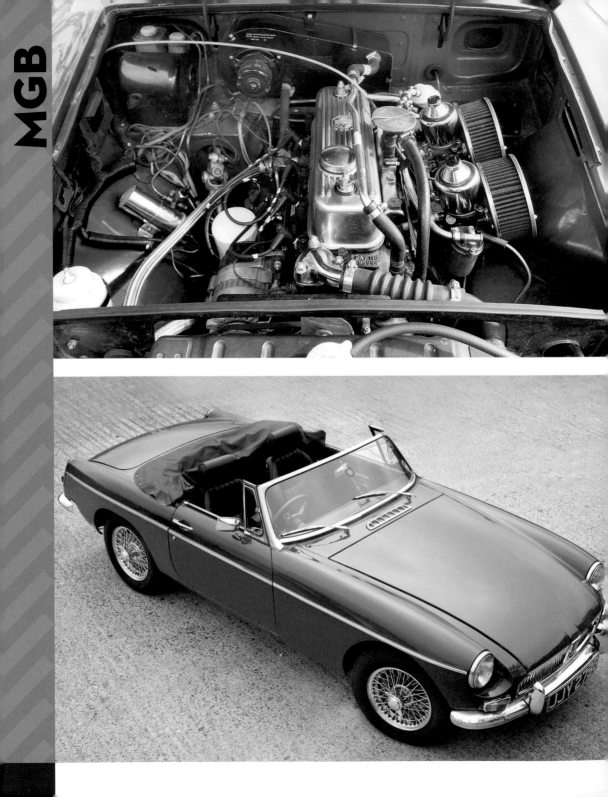

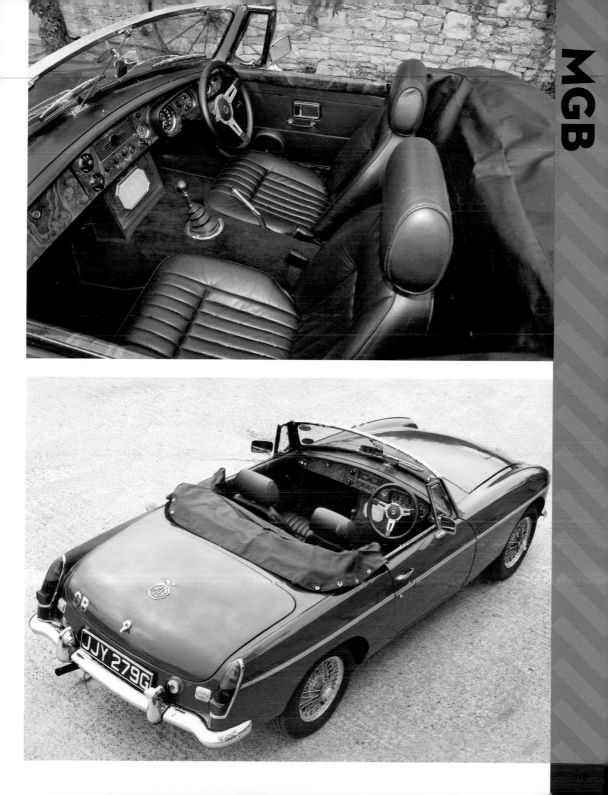

Penned by GM's Larry Shinoda, with inspiration from great designer Bill Mitchell's 1957 Stingray concept racer, the first Corvette coupe featured the iconic split rear window, pop-up headlights, and the new Sting Ray name. Gone was the X-frame from the earlier car, replaced with a new ladder chassis. The new Corvette was also equipped with an independent rear suspension for the first time, and the change improved handling.

Under the hood, the basic small-block 327 V-8 produced 250 horsepower. Buyers could select more potent options up to 360 horses

CORVETTE STING RAY 1963–1967

Country of manufacture: United States
Years of production: 1963 1967
Engine: 327–427-cubic-inch V-8
Output: 250–435 horsepower
Top speed: 140 miles per hour
Number built: 117,964

with higher compression and fuel injection. In 1965, the big-block option arrived with 425 horsepower on tap—and thankfully, so did four-wheel disc brakes. Maximum capacity for

the second-generation Corvette was reached in 1966 with the huge 427 V-8. Although it didn't develop much more power than its 396-cubic-inch predecessor, it had more torque.

In the cockpit, there was a short-shift gear level for the manual four-speed box, a twin-cowl dash featuring a large speedo' and rev counter in front of the driver, and flat panel seats. The Corvette's new radical shape won over the critics; the Sting Ray was so popular that the St. Louis factory where it was built initially had to work double shifts and still struggled to shorten a two-month waiting list for the cars.

Did You Know?

In 1962, while the Sting Ray was still on the drawing board, Zora Arkus-Duntov decided to build a special lightweight racer based on the new Corvette. The Grand Sport was to rival Shelby's Cobra and compete at Le Mans. With super-thin fiberglass panels, a lightweight frame, and a small-block motor with four Webers developing 550 horsepower, the car was very quick. Sadly the program was cancelled and only five cars were built.

CORVETTE STING RAY 1963-1967

FUEL INJECTION

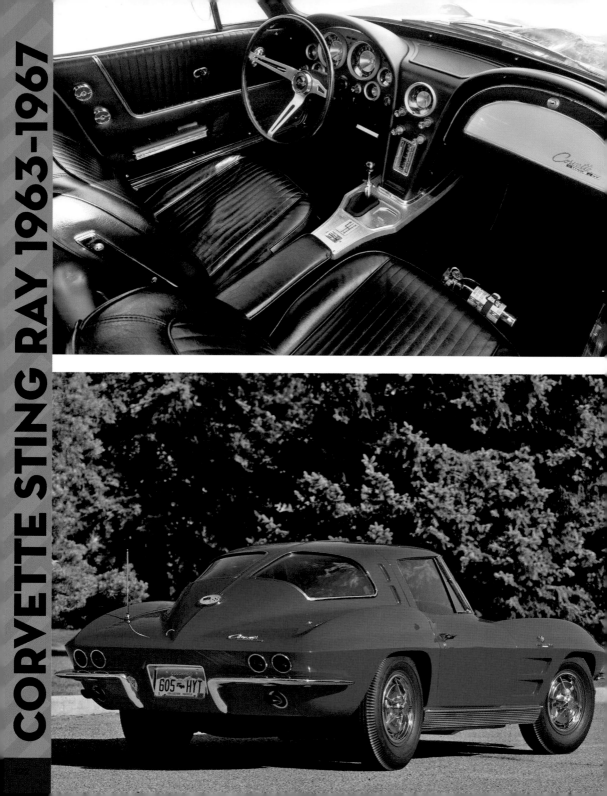

The stunning DB5 was one of the great aristocrats among sports cars of the 1960s. In 1963, a DB5 cost £4,562—enough to buy a decent-sized house or two Jaguar E-types. With Touring's beautifully designed alloy panels stretched over a *superleggera* framework of steel tubes built by Aston chief engineer Harold Beach, it became one of the most famous cars in the world due to its association with a certain British MI6 agent, James Bond.

The initials "DB" came from David Brown, who owned a tractor-making business before

ASTON MARTIN DB5

Country of manufacture: U.K.
Years of production: 1963–1965
Engine: 3,995cc DOHC straight six
Output: 314 horsepower (Vantage)
Top speed: 150 miles per hour (Vantage)
Number built: 1,021

acquiring both Aston Martin and Lagonda in 1947. He set about reorganizing the company, and there is still a solid evolution visible both in the design and engineering from Brown's first

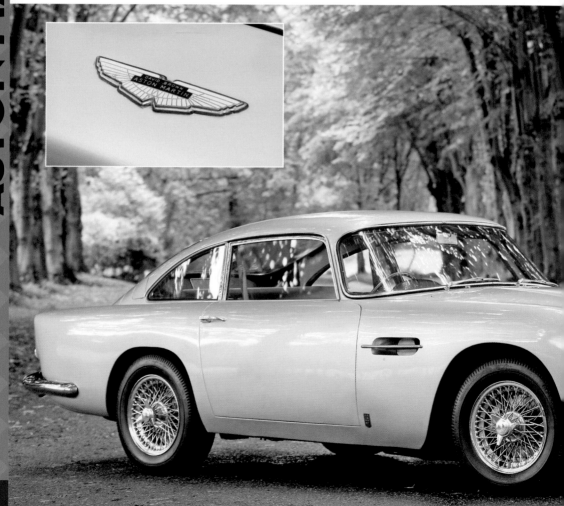

car up to the modern day. The DB5 featured the old Lagonda straight-six twin-cam engine, bored out to 4 liters with triple SU carburetors. In the Vantage version, these were replaced by triple Webers. An all-synchromesh five-speed ZF gearbox drove the car to an impressive 150 miles per hour in Vantage trim. High-speed testing was carried out on the brand-new, unrestricted M1 motorway a stone's throw from the factory in Newport Pagnell. Top-speed blasts from the elegant Aston are said to have contributed to a speed limit imposed on the motorway in 1964.

Inside, the DB5 was all walnut and leather, with electric windows as befitting a car of its price. Underneath, it had disc brakes all around and a slightly old-fashioned suspension with Armstrong adjustable lever-arm dampers and coil springs.

Did You Know?
Bought for $12,000 in 1969, the James Bond Aston Martin DB5 was sold at auction in 2010 for over $4 million.

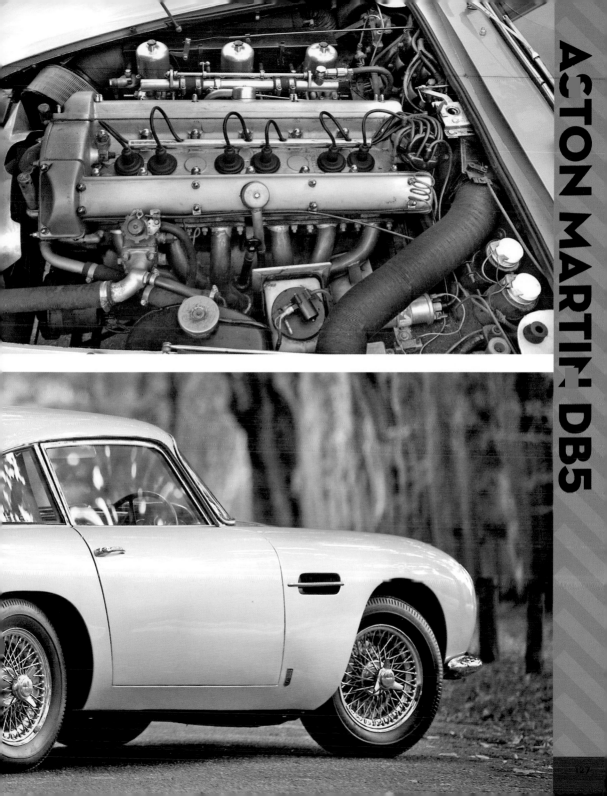

More luxurious than the rapidly aging 190SL it replaced, the 230SL had lots of modern options for 1963, including power steering, servo-assisted brakes, and an excellent automatic transmission. It was primarily built for the U.S. market, where most cars were sold, so Mercedes could tap urgently needed foreign currency.

Designed by Frenchman Paul Bracq, the SL came in roadster, 2+2, and coupe models. It was nicknamed the "Pagoda," due to its roof (when fitted) being higher at the sides than

MERCEDES 230/250/280SL

Country of manufacture: Germany
Years of production: 1963–1972
Engine: 2,281–2,778cc inline six
Output: 150–170 horsepower
Top speed: 127 miles per hour
Number built: 48,912

the middle. Initially the car featured the four main–bearing inline six-cylinder motor, but from the 250SL on, there was an even stronger

seven main–bearing crankshaft. The engine was matched with mechanical Bosch fuel injection developed for Formula 1, and a four- or five-speed manual or automatic gearbox.

Comfortable and safe, with independent rear suspension giving a firm ride and superb handling, the SL lacked some of the excitement of the Italian or British sports cars of the day but made up for it in reliability and build quality. This was well-proven in 1963, when a 230SL won the Marathon de la Route rally driven by Eugen Boringer, despite featuring disc brakes only on the front wheels. All-around discs came with the 250SL in 1967. The 280SL appeared just a year later and was superseded by the slab-sided and overweight 350SL in 1971.

Did You Know?

The SL stood for *super light*, although the 280SL was quite heavy compared to its more powerful cousin, the 300SL. It did have aluminum doors, hood, and trunk lid, however.

In the late 1950s, Jem Marsh and Frank Costin teamed up to build a sports car, combining their names to come up with the manufacturer's moniker. Their first design was the gawky, gull-winged GT, of which only 39 were built. The second try was the winner—a design penned by Denis Adams that has endured ever since in various incarnations. Initially built from lightweight marine plywood and fiberglass and available fully built or in kit form, the monocoque chassis received more traditional tubular steel construction in 1969. Power increased when builders turned from uninspired four-cylinder engines to the Volvo inline six or Ford V-6.

MARCOS 3.0 LITER

Country of manufacture: U.K.
Years of production: 1964–present
Engine: 1,498–4,999cc
Output: 82–352 horsepower
Top speed: 110–171 miles per hour
Number built: 1,500 approx.

Financial troubles in the 1970s forced the company to withdraw from sales of complete cars and concentrate on parts and service. Enough interest remained in the market to support introduction of an updated model in 1981. The timing was perfect—entering a market starved of sports cars, the two-seater coupe (and later spyder), now with Rover V-8 power, found immediate success. The fantastic Adams shape was still there under wider wheel arches, spoilers, and cowled-in headlights. The marque was brought up to date with such models as the Mantaray, and with a new company at the helm from 2002, the Marcos got its first complete, new body style since 1963.

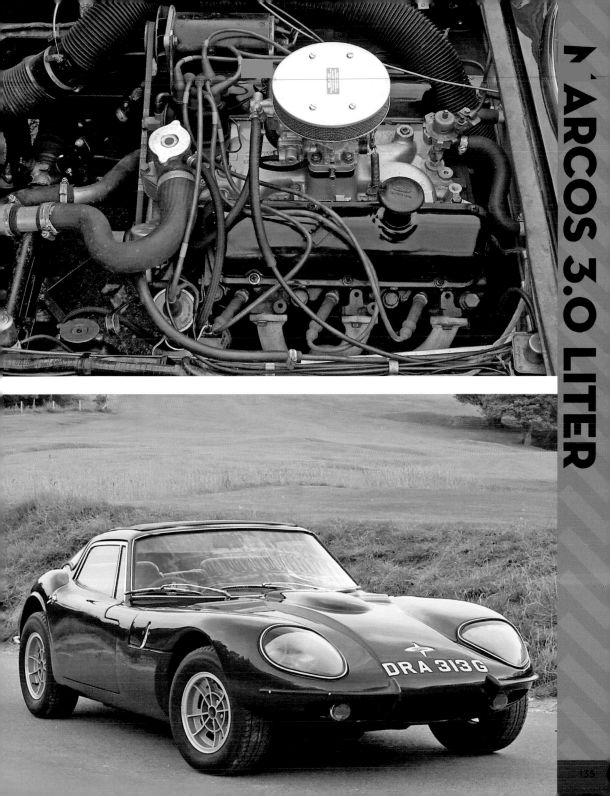

Named after Enzo Ferrari's favorite son, Alfre *dino*, who had died young in 1956, the Ferrari Dino shares its name and engine with the Fiat Dino. However, the Ferrari is mid-engined, with the motor mounted transversely (perpendicular to the frame). Enzo considered this to be a risky layout; he feared non-race drivers would find its handling challenging.

The Dino first appeared in 206S (2.0-liter) form at the 1966 Turin Auto Show, with a stunning Pininfarina alloy body around

FERRARI DINO 246GT

Country of manufacture: Italy
Years of production: 1969–1974
Engine: 2,418cc quad-cam V-6
Output: 195 horsepower
Top speed: 146 miles per hour
Number built: 3,912

a multi-tube frame and quad-cam engine. However, the model did not go on sale until 1968. A year later, the more powerful 246GT

shown here was introduced. Using a bigger 2.4-liter cast-iron block and triple Weber carburetors, it produced 195 horsepower—or 175 in the de-tuned U.S. version. Bodies on these cars were made of steel but were still built by Scaglietti. Beginning in 1971, a Targa top was offered in the GTS version.

Considered to be one of most beautiful postwar coupes ever built, the Dino also handled impeccably with independent suspension, coil springs, and discs brakes all around, balanced by a five-speed transmission mounted under the engine. The Dino introduced modern chassis design to Ferrari's model lineup.

Did You Know?

Although Dino Ferrari is often credited as creating the Dino V-6 engine, it was probably designed by Vittorio Jano, who effectively halved the much admired V-12 engine to make the first 1,500cc racing prototype, widening its angle from 60 to 65 degrees.

As a classic sports car, the Fiat Dino is often overlooked—and unfairly so. Often confused with the Ferrari of the same name, it shared the Dino engine with its more exotic cousin, but little else. The new Fiat Dino Spider was introduced at the Turin Auto Show in 1966 with a 2-liter engine and coachwork by Pininfarina. A Bertone-designed coupe arrived a year later. The early cars were built by Fiat in Turin.

FIAT DINO

Country of manufacture: Italy
Years of production: 1966–1973
Engine: 1,987cc or 2,418cc overhead quad-cam V-6
Output: 158–178 horsepower
Top speed: 130 miles per hour
Number built: 10,318

In 1969, a 2.4-liter iron-block Ferrari-type engine was offered, which increased output to nearly 180 horsepower. At the same time, the original live-axle and leaf-spring suspension was updated to an independent rear with coil springs. The Dino of this era used some components found on far more famous cars of the day, including the five-speed ZF gearbox used by Aston Martin and the same Girling brakes featured on the De Tomaso Pantera and Lamborghini Miura. By this time, the convertibles were being assembled along the same production line at Maranello as the Ferrari Dino. This was not a parts-bin sports car, but rather a product of clever badge engineering in difficult economic times.

Did You Know?

Dino Ferrari was never to see the great engine he helped to design. Enzo's son died of muscular dystrophy at the age of just 24 in 1956.

Ferruccio Lamborghini made his fortune building tractors and reconditioning military vehicles left over from World War II. Legend has it that he turned to making automobiles in response to a grudge against Enzo Ferrari, who treated Lamborghini rudely when he complained about the reliability of Ferrari's cars.

Lamborghini's first offerings were the 350GT and then 400GT—fairly standard, front-engined cars with styling by Touring. However, the P400, which later became the Miura, would prove to be a revolutionary design. First shown in rolling chassis form at the Turin Auto Show

LAMBORGHINI MIURA

Country of manufacture: Italy
Years of production: 1966–1972
Engine: 3,929cc quad-cam V-12
Output: 350–385 horsepower
Top speed: 170 miles per hour
Number built: 762

in 1965, it featured a mid-engined design previously seen in race cars but never before on a road car. Engineered by Gian Dallara and Giotto Bizzarrini, the new car was a steel monocoque structure with an all-aluminum

quad-cam V-12 engine mounted transversely behind the cockpit with a five-speed transaxle in unit to keep the length down. The Miura's styling was handed to Bertone's Marcello Gandini, who finished the prototype body just in time for the full car to appear at the 1966 Geneva show. The styling wowed crowds, and the orders began roll in despite the Miura's massive $20,000 price tag.

The engine featured a solid billet crank running on seven main bearings with four triple-choke Weber carburetors delivering explosive performance that was matched by the Miura's superb handling. The cabin, although hot and noisy, was suitably futuristic for 1966, with laid-back leather-paneled seats, a rev counter that went up to 10,000 rpm, and a speedometer numbered to an ambitious 200 miles per hour.

Lamborghini made several updates to the Miura during its six-year production run. The 1969 Miura S had a stiffer shell, improved suspension, wider tires, and vented disc brakes, while 1971 saw the arrival of the Miura SV with 385 horsepower on tap.

Did You Know?

The name Miura is Spanish for a fighting bull, which is featured on the emblem on the nose in direct challenge to Ferrari's prancing horse. The name is said to have come from Ferruccio Lamborghini's astrological sign, Taurus, the bull.

The twin-cam 275GTB was introduced at the 1964 Paris Motor Show. Built by coachbuilder Scaglietti for Ferrari, its gorgeous lines had been penned by Pininfarina yet again. Using the Colombo-designed 60-degree V-12, bored out to 3.3 liters with triple Weber carburetors, the 275 utilized a tubular frame with customers choosing either aluminum or standard steel panels. A transaxle transmission incorporated with the rear axle gave the Ferrari

a 50/50 weight balance to improve handling. Servo-assisted disc brakes were standard at all four corners.

In 1965, Ferrari produced a pure racer version called the 275GTC. Its resemblance to the GTB was only skin deep—the race car featured a new lightweight chassis, the 250LM motor, and ultra-thin alloy panels.

The GTB4 quad-cam V-12 arrived in 1966 with six twin-choke Weber carburetors and

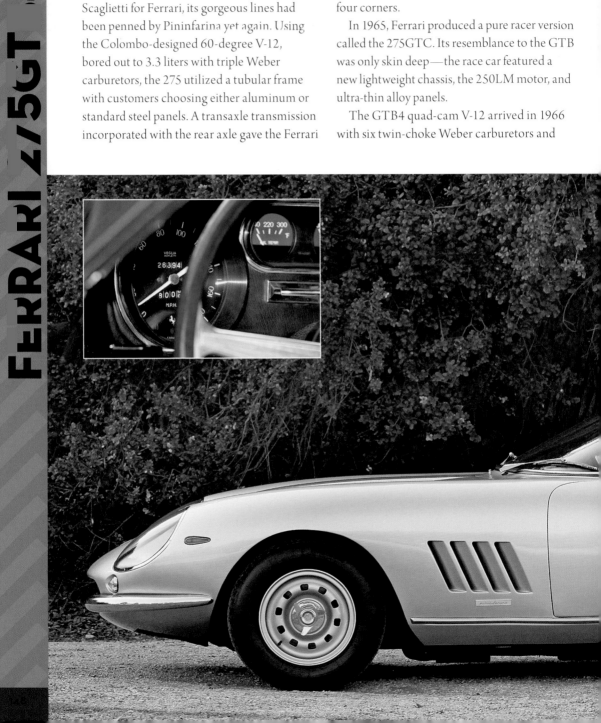

a dry-sump oil system—the kind usually found only in race cars, with a separate oil tank and no sump reservoir. The GTB4 was also more rigid, featuring a torque tube joining the engine and transaxle to stiffen the chassis and reduce vibration. For the first time on road-going cars, independent suspension appeared with double wishbones, coils springs, and telescopic shock absorbers.

FERRARI 275GTB4

Country of manufacture: Italy
Years of production: 1966–1968
Engine: 3,286cc quad-cam V-12
Output: 300 horsepower
Top speed: 165 miles per hour
Number built: 280

Did You Know?

The most exclusive 275GTB was the NART (North American Racing Team) Spider, commissioned by U.S. dealer Luigi Chinetti. Specially made by Scaglietti, each one cost $8,000. Only 10 were built.

The big step taken by its predecessor, the TR5 (TR250 in the U.S. market), was bringing in the smooth, inline-six engine from the Triumph 2000. The TR6 was mostly a styling update to the previous model, handled this time by Karmann.

A major difference divided the U.K. and U.S. variants: British-market cars made 150 horsepower with Lucas mechanical fuel injection, while their carbureted American kin

TRIUMPH TR6

Country of manufacture: U.K.
Years of production: 1968–1976
Engine: 2,498cc OHC inline six
Output: 150 horsepower (U.K. version),
   105 horsepower (U.S. version)
Top speed: 120 miles per hour
Number built: 94,619

put out only 105 horsepower. The reason for the change in the export models was stricter emissions laws in the United States.

Sticking to its separate-body-on-frame design spared the company extensive retooling for modern unit construction. Instead, the TR6 was the culmination of all previous Triumph developments and really benefited from it. There was independent suspension at the rear, precise rack-and-pinion steering, and a four-speed manual transmission with an optional overdrive, giving the car long legs on the freeway. The TR6 was so popular, particularly in the United States, that the Coventry factory found it hard to keep up with demand. Along with ample power, even in the States, it now had improved cockpit space and a better driving position, making the TR6 a great all-around sports car.

Did You Know?
Over 90 percent of all TR6s were sold outside of the U.K.

When it was first introduced at the 1968 Paris Motor Show, the 365GTB4 met with some disappointment from the press. They wanted to see a mid-engined Ferrari to take on the Lamborghini Miura, which was hoarding column inches at the time.

The 365 was to be the last and the fastest of the front-engined, rear-wheel-drive Ferraris until the 599 in 2006. Its nickname celebrated Ferrari's 1–2–3 finish in the 1967 24 Hours of Daytona race, which had been achieved with a 330P4. In fact, "Daytona" was an internal designation only, used during development;

but the name got leaked and it stuck, which infuriated Enzo Ferrari, who would only refer to the car as 365GTB4.

Designed by Leonardo Fioravanti at Pininfarina, the body was built by Scaglietti using the proven tubular frame technique with five-speed transaxle gearbox and torque tube at the back to spread the weight over the all-around independent suspension. Ferrari built 165 Spiders, which were designated 365GTS/4. A second series arrived in 1971 with retractable headlights instead of the fixed ones, mounted in the nose under acrylic

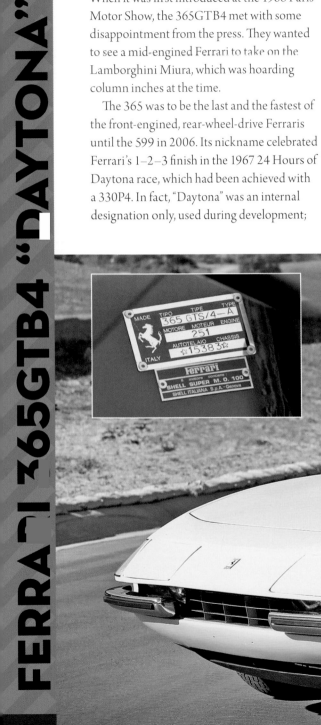

glass. The engine was the all-alloy, dry-sump Colombo V-12, featuring six twin-choke Webers and putting out an impressive 352 horsepower at 7,500 rpm.

Three series of competition cars were built, in 1971, 1972, and 1973, with lightweight aluminum panels strengthened by fiberglass and plexiglass windows. The race engine was tuned to a maximum output of 450 horsepower. Raced by privateers, the competition cars were especially effective at Le Mans in 1972, where they took the first five places in the GT class.

FERRARI 365GTB4 "DAYTONA"

Country of manufacture: Italy
Years of production: 1968–1974
Engine: 4,390cc quad-cam V-12
Output: 352 horsepower
Top speed: 174 miles per hour
Number built: 1,285

Did You Know?

In 1971, Dan Gurney and Brock Yates drove a Daytona coast to coast from New York to Los Angeles in 35 hours and 54 minutes in the inaugural Cannonball Run.

FERRARI 365 GTB4 "DAYTONA"

CHAPTER 4
THE AGE OF THE ENTHUSIAST: THE 1970s, '80s, AND '90s

The 1970s and '80s were tough times for the sports car, especially the British models. Car manufacturing in the U.K. was on its knees amid mergers and shutdowns. Many famous names closed their doors, including Riley, Triumph, Austin, and MG.

Some small carmakers weathered the storm, such as Morgan with its Plus 8 model and Lotus with the Esprit. In mainland Europe, Porsche stuck its neck out with its first ever front-engined cars, the 924 and 928, but in the end it would be the 911 that saw the company through.

In the United States, cars just got bigger, reflecting greater affluence. Yet more stringent federal emission controls made it more difficult for the European sports car manufacturers to tap the world's largest car market. Many either stopped their exports or went out of business.

Amidst all the doom and gloom, Fiat and Ferrari created some of their best sports cars. The 124 Spider was the biggest seller, enduring for nearly 20 years; at the other end of the spectrum, the F40 proved a masterpiece of minimalist race car engineering, good for 200 miles per hour on the open road.

Meanwhile, in the East, Japanese carmakers were producing high-volume products of increasing quality, unaffected by (or perhaps capitalizing on) the troubles of the Old World. They looked back at the great designs of the past and wondered how to make them work in the current climate. It could be said that this kind of thinking culminated in the sensational rebirth of the classic sports car in the form of the Mazda MX-5 Miata. Its arrival in 1989 was a revelation: an affordable and highly enjoyable roadster that looked every part the classic MG or Lotus, but featuring the latest technology.

A stunning mid-engined Giugiaro wedge-shaped design based around a steel backbone, the Esprit featured a fiberglass body with all-independent suspension and disc brakes. As with many other modern sports cars of the time, the Esprit's 2-liter, four-cylinder, 16-valve motor was mounted longitudinally behind the driver. In typical Lotus fashion, the car's components came from the parts bins of other manufacturers: the transaxle gearbox came from the Citroën SM; the steering rack from the Triumph Herald; the taillights from the Fiat X1/9. It was still

LOTUS ESPRIT

Country of manufacture: U.K.
Years of production: 1976–2004
Engine: 2-liter inline four, up to 5-liter V-8
Output: 160 horsepower (inline four), up to 349 horsepower (5-liter V-8)
Top speed: 135–175 miles per hour
Number built: 10,675

a striking-looking car with enough cachet to appear in a fabulous car chase in the 1977 James Bond movie, *The Spy Who Loved Me.*

In 1980, Lotus launched an updated version, the S2.2, which featured a bigger, turbocharged engine. The new 210-horsepower motor required a stiffer chassis and a revised suspension; these changes would create the sweetest-handling Esprit of all. Designer Peter Stevens softened the lines in 1987, making the car even more aerodynamic, and there was another restyling in 1993.

By 1996, the Esprit was more than 20 years old and needed something more to compete with the likes of Ferrari and Porsche. That something came in the form of a brand-new Lotus-developed twin-turbo V-8, which kicked out a massive 349 horsepower and boosted the car's top speed to over 170 miles per hour. The last Esprit finally rolled off the production line in Hethel in February 2004, but a new-generation Esprit was announced in 2010 and is set to arrive on the streets in spring 2013.

Did You Know?

The underwater Esprit that appeared in *The Spy Who Loved Me* was built from a standard car by Perry Submarines of Florida. With four thrusters added to its tail, the sub was capable of nearly 15 knots.

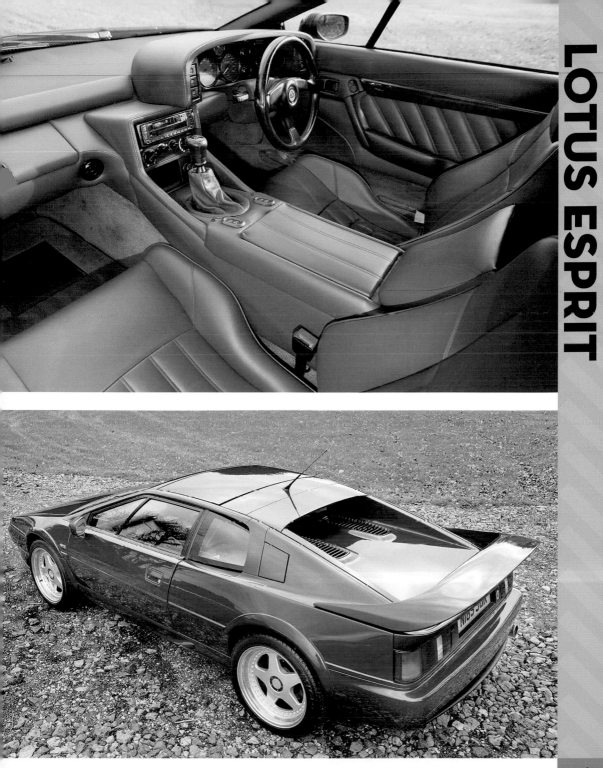

A production run of nearly 20 years makes this Fiat one of the most successful sports cars ever, certainly in terms of overall sales. Launched at the 1966 Turin Auto Show, the design was pure Pininfarina, and the Italian coachbuilder would manufacture the 124's monocoque bodies throughout the car's run.

Ex-Ferrari chief engineer Aurelio Lampredi designed the car's innovative series of engines, which initially had a pair of twin-choke Weber carburetors and, later, Bosch fuel injection feeding an aluminum crossflow head with dual overhead camshafts driven by reinforced

FIAT 124 SPORT SPIDER

Country of manufacture: Italy
Years of production: 1966–1985
Engine: 1,138–1,995cc DOHC inline four-cylinder
Output: 135 horsepower
(supercharged 2.0-liter model)
Top speed: 120 miles per hour
Number built: 198,000

rubber belts. Gearboxes were four- or five-speed manual units with a three-speed automatic for the U.S. market. Braking was provided via discs all around, and the 124 had conventional coil

suspension, except on the Abarth model, which used a fully independent rear axle.

Fiat began entering the 124 Sport Spider in rallies in 1970 but enjoyed little success until they handed over the program to Abarth; in 1972, the car finished second overall in the Rallye Monte Carlo and won the driver's championship. These rally spiders always ran with a hardtop and continued to be successful until 1976 when they were replaced by the Fiat 131. The road-going 124 Abarth Rallye was the homologation special. Built in low numbers, it is both rare and desirable. Other variants included a turbo version for the States and a supercharged model for Europe, which delivered the most power of all the production cars. For the last three years of the 124's production run, Fiat handed the whole car over to Pininfarina, which sold it under the 2000 Spider or Spidereuropa badges.

Did You Know?
The Fiat 124 Abarth's best rally result came in the Rally of Portugal in 1974, where 124s swept the podium with a 1–2–3 finish.

B687 AMH

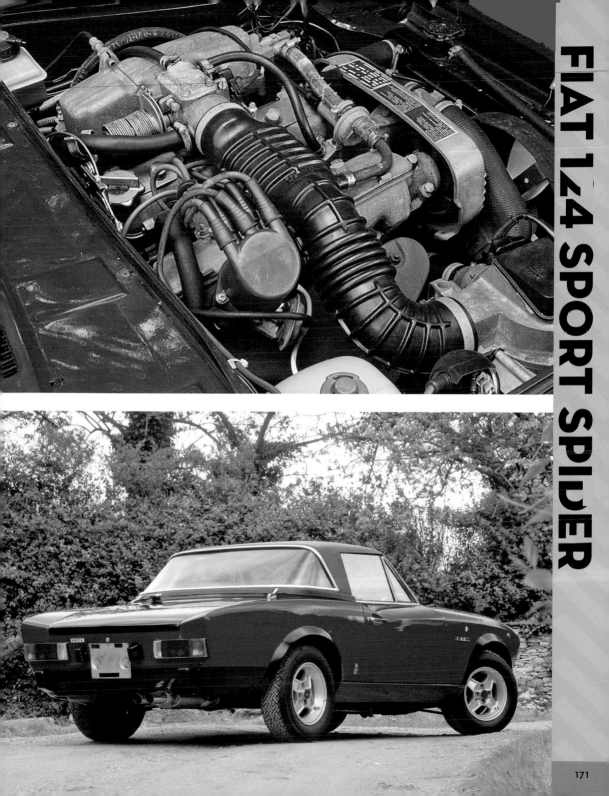

The 308 replaced the Dino 246 in 1975 even though a similarly named Bertone-designed car, the Dino 308GT4, had been launched a few years earlier.

Ferrari went back to Pininfarina for the 308 GTB/GTS design, but the car ran on the same mechanics as the GT4 with a dry-sump, two-cam, mid-engined V-8 mounted transversely behind the driver, ahead of the rear wheels. A limited-slip differential and five-speed transaxle were tucked in behind it; fuel was fed to the motor by four Weber carburetors. The first cars were built using fiberglass panels to keep the weight down, but this was abandoned in 1977, at which point the bodywork was made of steel.

The GTS, with its Targa-style top, outsold the closed GTB by a large margin, and the 308 enjoyed soaring sales, particularly in the United States. The replacement of Weber carburetors for fuel injection in 1981 spoiled the power for about 18 months before a four-valve-per-cylinder (Quattrovalvole) head brought it back. In 1980, Ferrari introduced a 208 model for markets such as Italy and New Zealand, where

special tax concessions were made for cars with engine displacements under 2 liters. At 1,991cc and just 155 horsepower, the 208 was somewhat underwhelming and only about 300 were built. For 1986, these little V-8s received a boost from turbochargers, bringing their output up to 254 horsepower.

The 328 edition, as shown here, arrived in 1985 and featured a bored-out motor and 270 horsepower on tap. Ferrari built almost 20,000 of the 308/328GTB/GTS line, making it one of the company's most successful cars.

FERRARI 308/328GTB/GTS

Country of manufacture: Italy
Years of production: 1985–1989 (328 shown here)
Engine: 2,926cc (308), 3,185cc (328) DOHC V-8
Output: 214–270 horsepower
Top speed: 140–160 miles per hour
Number built: 19,555 (includes 308 and 328GTB/GTS)

Did You Know?

The 308/328's long-running success was no doubt helped by its prominence in the popular 1980s TV series *Magnum P.I.* A red 308 was the preferred choice of transportation for title character Thomas Magnum's adventures in the Hawaiian Islands. In fact, Magnum (played by Tom Selleck) drove three different 308GTSs during the series, starting with a straight 308GTS before moving on to the fuel-injected GTSi and finishing with the GTSi QV.

The 911 is one of the truly legendary models in sports car history. Porsche's rear-engined, rear-wheel-drive stalwart has been in continuous production for nearly a half century and shows no sign of slipping today. Designed in the early 1960s as a replacement for the 356 model, the 911 featured styling by Butzi Porsche; its engine received an additional pair of cylinders but remained in air-cooled, flat, horizontally opposed form. Initially equipped with Weber carburetors, these were substituted with Solexes in 1966 before fuel injection appeared in 1969. As it has throughout the car's run, Porsche built a range of models at this time, including a coupe, Targa, Carrera, and a hot 911S, which featured high-compression pistons and ventilated disc brakes. Right from the start, Porsche began to prove the capabilities of its great-handling sports car in competition, and 911s would win the Monte Carlo Rally in 1968, 1969, and 1970.

Over the decades, Porsche has continued to develop and evolve the 911, always keeping it at the cutting edge of sports car technology. In

the mid-1970s, Porsche added a turbocharger to the 3.0-liter engine, offering exhilarating acceleration for those brave enough to push the pedal all the way down. These 911 Turbos sported a huge "whale tail" spoiler that changed the car's look, though for better or worse is a subject of debate.

On the track, Porsche won again at Le Mans in 1979 with the factory racing version of the 911 Turbo, the 935. It also dominated sports car racing that year, winning at Daytona, Sebring, and the Nürburgring 1,000 km. In fact, 911s are ubiquitous at sports car racing events and numerous international racing series. The four-wheel-drive Carrera 4 arrived in 1989 using technology from Porsche's 1984 Paris-Dakar Rally winner. In 1998, the air-cooled engine reached the end of its long service and development, replaced with a brand-new water-cooled unit. Body styling was updated at the same time. The latest 911 revision came in 2005, keeping the car's image up to date, an image associated with advanced performance technology without being too flashy.

PORSCHE 911

Country of manufacture: Germany
Years of production: 1963–present
Engine: 1,991–3,800cc DOHC horizontally opposed six
Output: 130–473 horsepower (997 Turbo)
Top speed: 130–194 miles per hour
Number built: 700,000 (all models through January 2010)

Did You Know?

The 3-liter Carrera RS Lightweight of 1973 is considered to be the ultimate early 911. Only 59 of these 230-horsepower cars were built. Originally priced at $11,000, they are valued at $250,000 to $350,000 today.

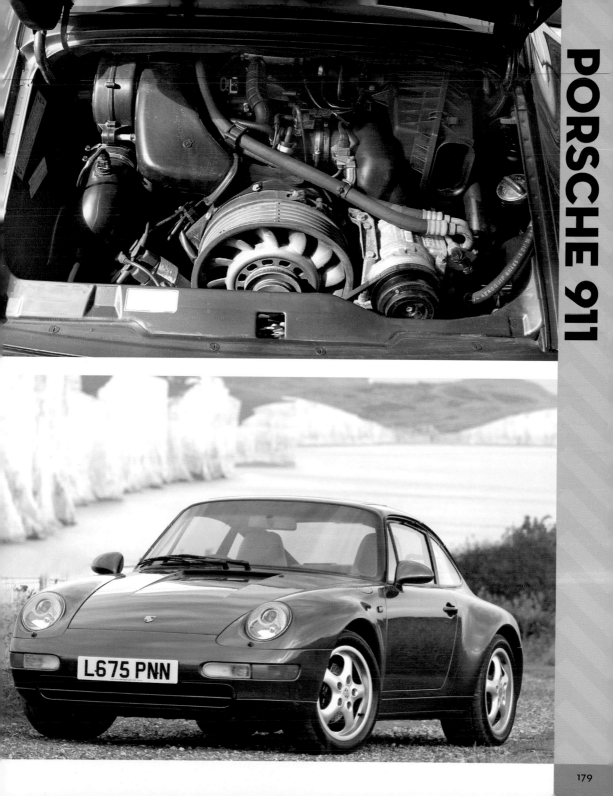

During negotiations with Rover to buy Morgan in 1967, Peter Morgan heard about Rover acquiring a new Buick-derived, all-alloy V-8 engine. Despite the buyout not going forward, Morgan asked if he could get a supply of the new motor. Rover agreed and Morgan set about shoehorning it into the Plus 4, which he did by widening the wings to accommodate bigger tires and lengthening the chassis. The potent result was the Plus 8, which would carry Morgan through the difficult times ahead for the U.K. motor industry.

MORGAN PLUS 8

Country of manufacture: U.K.
Years of production: 1968–2004
Engine: Rover 3,528/3,916/1,522cc overhead V-8
Output: 165–225 horsepower
Top speed: 125 miles per hour
Number built: More than 6,000

Owners loved the tail-happy, powerful car with its sweet-handling chassis, lightweight frame, all-alloy panels, and throaty exhaust note. However, prospective buyers faced a long

wait in getting the car, as only a dozen emerged from the Malvern works each week.

The Plus 8 is the fastest ever Morgan and could beat a Jaguar E-type off the line and accelerate to 90 miles per hour quicker than a Porsche. With its blend of modern power, close-ratio five-speed gearbox (from 1977), and good old-fashioned style, it was a life saver for the company.

Between 1974 and 1992, all Plus 8s exported to the United States were converted to run on propane gas to meet the stringent federal emission laws, and it was only after Rover recertified the V-8 that normal service resumed. With Rover's development of the V-8 engine into 3.9- and 4.6-liter capacities, power climbed to over 220 horsepower when the final cars rolled out of the factory in 2004.

Did You Know?

To mark the 35th year of production of its Plus 8, Morgan produced an Anniversary Edition with a special trim features. Yet due to the firm's long waiting list, most buyers didn't receive their cars until 2004, when the model was 36 years old!

Named for Ferrari's 40th anniversary, the F40 was the last car commissioned by Enzo Ferrari before his death in 1988. Based on the 288GT0 platform and sharing much of the engineering of the "Evoluzione" race car, the F40 made innovative use of composite materials for weight reduction. With this in mind, the cabin was Spartan like a racer, with exposed carbon fiber and no carpets or door trim. The windows and windscreen were even made of plastic.

FERRARI F40

Country of manufacture: Italy
Years of production: 1987–1992
Engine: 2,936cc twin-turbo V-8
Output: 478 horsepower
Top speed: 201 miles per hour
Number built: 1,315

The 3-liter twin-turbocharged V-8 was a screamer, offering up more than 475 horsepower—with another 200 horsepower

available if you ordered the racing version. The chassis featured a central composite section with steel tubular frames at each end to support the very stiff but adjustable independent suspension. There was a huge molded rear wing integral to the back end (much copied by other designers in later years) and a clear vented plexiglass engine cover so you could see the beast within. Its race pedigree was further enhanced by three-piece wheels, group C brakes, and bag-type fuel cells.

Intended to compete with the Porsche 959, the F40 was much lighter and had better performance, outrunning the German supercar's top speed by 4 miles per hour.

Did You Know?
The F40 was the first production car to break the 200-mile-per-hour barrier and could go from 0 to 100 miles per hour in just 7.8 seconds.

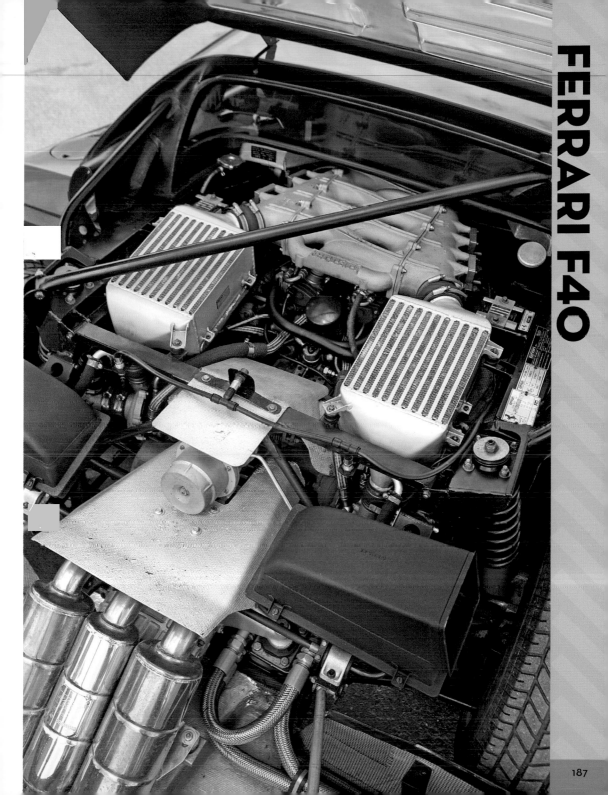

As with the Ferrari Testarossas of decades past, the 1980s Testarossas were so named for the color of the cam covers on their 48-valve dry-sump 12-cylinder Boxer engines. The car inherited much of its engineering from the Berlinetta Boxer, which had first appeared in the early 1970s, but with a number of differences: To save weight, the bodywork was crafted out of aluminum, except for the doors and roof. Its slippery and controversial shape was the result of a great deal of time in the wind-tunnel by Pininfarina. From the outside, the Testarossa

FERRARI TESTAROSSA 512TR

Country of manufacture: Italy
Years of production: 1984–1996
Engine: 4,943cc 48-valve flat 12
Output: 441 horsepower
Top speed: 190 miles per hour
Number built: 9,973

512TR was miles away from the civilized lines of the understated Boxer.

The Testarossa was tremendously wide due to its huge flat 12's mid-engine position and

flared wheel arches, along with a much roomier cabin. Twin radiators were positioned in front of the rear wheels and were fed air through the distinctive cooling vents that started along the doors.

As expected from a Ferrari, the car provided impressive performance, going from 0 to 60 miles per hour in just 5.5 seconds and powering up to an incredible top speed of over 180 miles per hour. Yet maneuvering the car at slower speeds was tricky, and its shapely design offered poor visibility for the driver. Like its predecessor, it had all-around independent suspension but now with 40/60 front–rear weight distribution.

In 1992, Ferrari renamed it the 512TR, tweaked the engine for more power, improved the gearbox, and lowered the ride height. Ferrari was trying to reclaim the unofficial best supercar title from its old rival Lamborghini, which had launched the Diablo a year earlier. The final incarnation of the car was the F512M. Released in 1994 with more engine upgrades, its top speed approached 200 miles per hour.

Did You Know?

The only official Testarossa Spider (convertible) was made as a gift for Fiat boss Gianni Agnelli in 1986 and featured a silver Ferrari logo in place of the standard aluminum version.

It's not an exaggeration to say that the Mazda MX-5 Miata reinvented the small sports car. It arrived at a time when there was little competition in the market and took its cues from the classic British models of the 1960s, such as the MGB, Lotus Elan, and Austin-Healey.

The first generation (or Mk. 1) was a simple, lightweight, front-engined, rear-wheel-drive machine capable of meeting the strict emission and safety requirements that had killed off many of the traditional sports cars. Early styling work was done by International Automotive

MAZDA MX-5 MIATA (FIRST GENERATION)

Country of manufacture: Japan
Years of production: 1989–1998 (first generation)
Engine: 1.6- or 1.8-liter DOHC inline four
Output: 115–133 horsepower
Top speed: 130 miles per hour
Number built: 421,322

Design (IAD) in Britain. The car was clothed in an all-steel body, except for the aluminum hood, and featured distinctive pop-up headlights. Its shape evolved after a competition between

California- and Tokyo-based Mazda design teams, as well as feedback from thousands of American enthusiasts.

Its engine and five-speed gearbox was mounted longitudinally, giving the car its perfectly balanced 50/50 front-to-rear weight ratio. All-wheel disc brakes and independent suspension supplemented the Miata's neutral handling. Two powerplants were offered—both DOHC inline fours of either 1.6 or 1.8 liters. They were mounted low in the monocoque and featured fuel injection and electronic ignition. Mazda even developed the exhaust note to a nostalgic bark rather than the quieter purr it would have produced otherwise.

The first-generation MX-5 was an immediate success. Mazda sold more than 400,000 units in the car's first nine years of production, while at the same time spawning a huge community of enthusiasts, with hundreds of MX-5 Miata clubs all over the world.

Did You Know?

In 2000, the *Guinness Book of World Records* declared the MX-5 Miata the best-selling two-seat convertible sports car in the world.

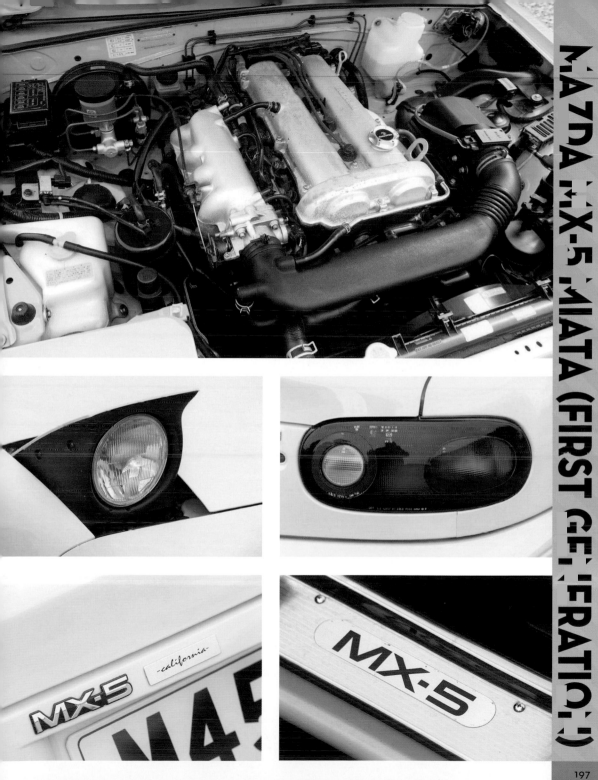

Back in 1988, Chrysler president Bob Lutz called on his company to build a modern sports car along the lines of the much-admired Shelby Cobra, with its powerful engine and simple styling. Chrysler even brought in Cobra originator Carroll Shelby to influence the early design of the car. The results were shown in the form of a concept car at the North American Auto Show in 1989; it produced such a buzz that Chrysler chairman Lee Iacocca soon gave his approval to build a production version.

Power was to come from Chrysler's V-10 engine, which was produced at the time for trucks. But it was too heavy in its iron-block form, so Chrysler's subsidiary Lamborghini was tasked with recasting it in aluminum alloy. The Viper's body was paneled in lightweight fiberglass around a tubular steel frame.

The first preproduction car was driven by Shelby as a pace car at the 1991 Indianapolis 500. It was fast but not very sophisticated, lacking wind-up windows or a hardtop roof; it also lacked some of the safety additions that were often standard on performance cars of the day, such as anti-lock brakes and traction control.

In 1996, Chrysler launched the second-generation Viper. Called the GTS, it featured a low-line coupe roof with a double bubble that provided additional clearance for drivers to be able to wear racing helmets. Again, Shelby was involved in early stages, and the new car had a noticeable resemblance to the Peter Brock–designed Daytona Cobra of the 1960s. On track it was not a car for the faint-hearted, but it was successfully raced in its GTRS form at the 24 Hours of Le Mans and the 24 Hours of Daytona; it also won the FIA GT championship three times.

In 2003, a restyled car appeared called the Viper SRT-10, which featured a more pronounced front with angled headlights and a bigger, 500-horsepower engine. The extra horsepower increased top speed in the coupe version to 192 miles per hour. The fourth-generation cars built from 2008 to 2010 were capable of over 200 miles per hour. In 2010, Chrysler mooted its intentions of launching a fifth-generation Viper in 2012.

DODGE VIPER RT/10

Country of manufacture: United States
Years of production: 1992–1995 (first generation)
Engine: aluminum-alloy V-10
Output: 400 horsepower (first generation)
Top speed: 180 miles per hour
Number built: 25,000 (all generations)

Did You Know?

Among the initial criteria for building the first Viper was that it could travel from 0 to 100 miles per hour and back to 0 in under 15 seconds.

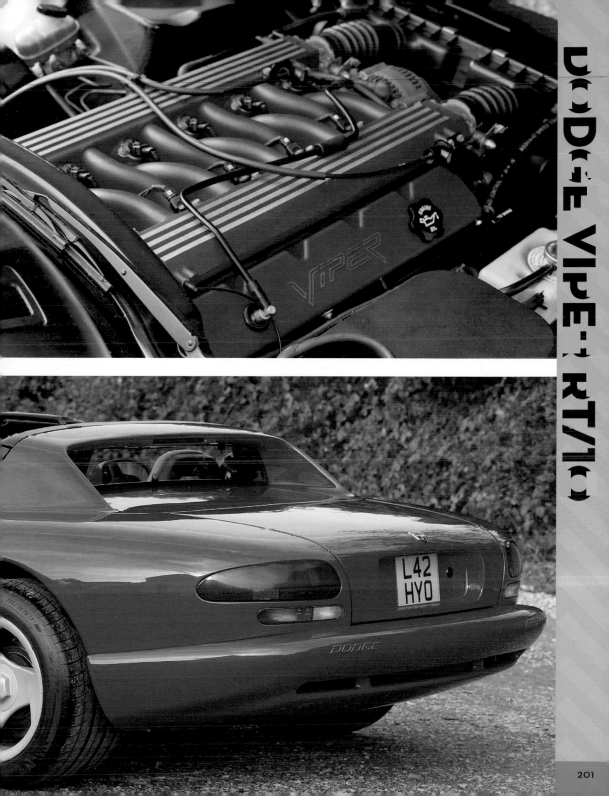

One of the best basic sports cars ever conceived, the Lotus Elise ticks all the boxes—lightweight, great-looking, and one of the best power-to-weight ratios ever built in a production car. It is a true successor to the Lotus Seven. Mid-engined and rear-wheel drive, it was a huge improvement over the front-drive, front-engined Elan that Lotus had produced just five years earlier. Designed by Julian Thomson, the Elise gets much of its superb go kart–like handling from the rigidity of its monocoque chassis, which is built from extruded and bonded aluminum clothed in thin fiberglass panels. The Elise's suspension is so good that it needs no anti-roll bars, though it does give a stiff ride.

Early models of the Elise came with the rather mild-mannered Rover K-series engine, which kicked out just 120 horsepower; but this was enough power to produce a 0-to-60 time of just over five seconds, thanks to the fact that the Elise carries half the weight of a family hatchback. Numerous special editions have been made, including the 111S with an improved engine, a closer-ratio gearbox, and various other upgrades; the roofless and doorless 340R; and the hardtop Exige.

In 2002, Lotus began offering the Series II, a computer-designed evolution that met the E.U.'s increasingly stringent laws. In 2004, the Elise finally went on sale officially in the United States, after receiving an exemption from bumper and headlight regulation. Its new engine was an aluminum Toyota block with a Yamaha-designed, twin-cam, variable valve timing head mated to a manual six-speed transmission. In 2010, a Series III Elise concept appeared at the Paris Motor Show, signaling the shape of things to come.

LOTUS ELISE

Country of manufacture: U.K.
Years of production: 1996–present
Engine: 1,598–1,975cc inline four
Output: 120–217 horsepower
Top speed: 150 miles per hour (supercharged version)
Number built: 20,000+ (through 2009)

Did You Know?

The Lotus Elise platform has spawned a number of other sports cars, including the electric-drive Tesla Roadster, Vauxhall VX220/Opel Speedster, electric-drive Dodge Circuit EV, and, weirdest of all, the Rinspeed sQuba, a submarine version launched in 2008. Inspired by the amphibious Esprit from the James Bond movie *The Spy Who Loved Me*, the sQuba is powered by three electric motors and can run on land as well as below the surface, with propulsion provided by wheels, propeller, and water jet.

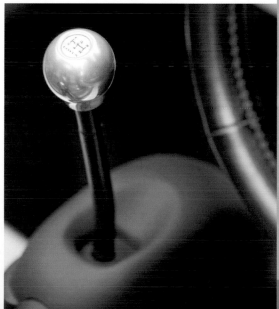

CHAPTER 5
TWENTY-FIRST-CENTURY SPORTS CARS

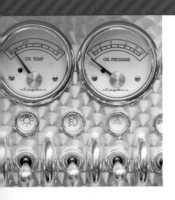

The 1990s ended on a high, with economies on the rise and automakers' order books brimming. The state of affairs encouraged companies such as Audi, who had never built a sports car, to dip its toes in the market with the TT. Similarly, Honda, who had not produced a true sports car since the S600 and S800 models back in the late 1960s, unveiled the S2000 to great acclaim.

In a reversal from the 1980s, when names were disappearing, some were now coming back—at least in prototype form—such as Connaught, Frazer Nash, and Spyker, which produced the extraordinary C8. Smart, a spin-off from luxury brand Mercedes, produced an excellent small sports car that encompassed all of the build quality and ethos of its larger and more expensive big brother.

Aston Martin and Jaguar had benefited greatly from joint ownership by Ford in the 1990s and had even been successful on the track with the DBR9GT, placing them in a pole position for surviving the tough times ahead.

By 2008, the bubble of economic optimism in the West had burst, leaving the developing markets in a more competitive position to support the Old World. Rather than consumers in the United States and Europe buying sports cars, the market had expanded to include India, China, and Brazil, as well as a host of emerging economies. Meanwhile, new technologies and hybrid systems such as hydrogen fuel cells and pure electric cars were coming on strong, yielding exciting future prospects like the fantastically fast Tesla. And Ferrari, long regarded as the epitome of a sports car manufacturer, launched the California in 2008, almost 50 years to the day since the 250GT Spyder of the same name appeared.

Introduced at the Geneva Motor Show in 2003, the V-8 Vantage is conceptually a direct descendent of the DBS V-8 from the late 1960s, whose powerplant endured throughout the 1970s, 1980s, and 1990s in a range of Aston Martin cars before finally being discontinued in 2000. When production of the new Vantage began in 2005, Aston Martin and Jaguar were both owned by Ford, and the new car was initially powered by a 4.3-liter engine derived from the Jaguar AJ26 V-8. Since 2008, V-8 Vantages have used an all-alloy, AM 4.7-liter,

ASTON MARTIN V-8 VANTAGE

Country of manufacture: U.K.
Years of production: 2005–present
Engine: 4,735cc quad-cam V-8
Output: 420 horsepower
Top speed: 180 miles per hour
Number built: 15,000

32-valve, quad-cam motor assembled in Cologne, Germany. With the dry-sump engine set low in the chassis to improve the center of gravity and a transaxle transmission, the

Vantage has a near-perfect 49/51 front–rear balance. This strong platform has served as the basis for several other Aston Martin models: the DBS, DB9, V-12 Vantage, and Rapide are also hand-built on these same underpinnings.

The Vantage's body structure is made of bonded aluminum, which provides both lightness and strength. A six-speed manual or Sportshift sequential gearbox is available, as well as leather upholstery for the seats, dash, steering wheel, and shift knob. In 2006, Aston Martin introduced a Roadster variant, which gained some weight due to a chassis-stiffening crossmember but with no loss of top speed. Power-assisted rack-and-pinion steering and independent suspension all around give the V-8 Vantage the precise and responsive handling of a classic in the making.

Did You Know?

Before Aston Martin opened its new plant at Gaydon, Warwickshire, England, in 2003, all Aston Martins were hand-made in a small works in Newport Pagnell. The old plant rolled out its last car, a Vanquish S, on July 19, 2007, after nearly 13,000 cars had been made there since 1955. The Tickford Street factory remains the Aston Martin restoration and service department.

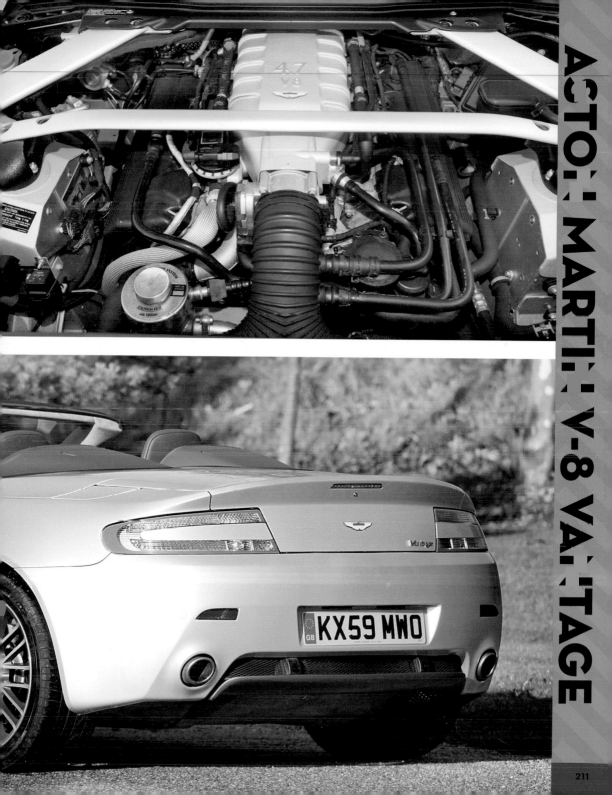

The Honda S2000 was created to celebrate the company's 50 years as a car manufacturer; its name was chosen as a nod to the very first Honda cars, the S500, S600, and S800, and the numbers designate the models' engine displacement in cubic centimeters. First unveiled as a concept designed by Shigeru Uehara at the 1995 Tokyo Motor Show, the rear-wheel-drive monocoque sports car was built on a very rigid X-bone frame. The car's 50/50 weight distribution was facilitated by

HONDA S2000
Country of manufacture: Japan
Years of production: 1999–2009
Engine: 1,997cc DOHC inline four
Output: 237 horsepower
Top speed: 150 miles per hour
Number built: 112,631

mounting the engine behind the front axle. Very high spec from the start, the torquey, 2-liter, normally aspirated, dual-overhead-cam,

16-valve four-cylinder engine featured Honda's excellent V-TEC variable valve timing system, which allows it to rev to nearly 9,000 rpm.

The production car came equipped with a six-speed manual transmission pushing its 237 horsepower to the wheels via a Torsen limited-slip differential. A push-button starter awakened the engine. In 2004, the S2000 received a facelift and its engine capacity was increased to 2.2 liters, though power was limited by a cut-out at 8,200 rpm. In 2006, a drive-by-wire system was introduced to the throttle layout and electronic stability control was added for safety. Much loved by both critics and owners, the S2000 did not sell in terrific numbers, and in the wake of the economic recession, Honda decided to discontinue to model in 2009.

Did You Know?
Soichiro Honda's first car, the S500 of 1963, was chain-driven owing to his background in motorcycle design.

The Tesla Roaster has been the most exciting car to emerge from the many new-technology hybrids and alternative-energy vehicles that have appeared in recent years. Built by Tesla Motors in California, the Roadster greatly resembles a Lotus Elise and does in fact share some parts with the British marque. But under its carbon-fiber skin lies a hugely powerful air-cooled electric motor that produces the equivalent of nearly 300 horsepower, provides blistering acceleration of 0 to 60 in 3.7 seconds, and exceeds 125 miles per hour.

TESLA ROADSTER

Country of manufacture: United States
Years of production: 2008–present
Engine: 375-volt, three-phase, four-pole induction electric motor
Output: 288 horsepower
Top speed: 125 miles per hour
Number built: 1,200 (through July 2010)

As with the Elise, the Roadster chassis is a resin-bonded and riveted aluminum monocoque, which makes it both flexible and

immensely strong. Its rigidity is enhanced by using the battery pack as a stressed member. The pack, or Energy Storage System (ESS), is made up of 6,831 lithium ion cells, similar to the kind used in laptops. It is charged via a home connector or through a regenerative braking system, as used in current Formula 1 cars. In tests, the car can travel up to 244 miles on a single charge, which should only cost about $4.

The rear wheels are driven via a single-speed fixed gearbox built by Borg Warner at a ratio of 8:28:1. To take the huge torque, the power delivered to the road is managed by traction control, anti-lock braking system (ABS), and four-wheel vented discs. All this fantastic technology comes at a price though—$109,000 (£86,950).

Did You Know?

Tesla takes its name from the Serbian electrical engineer, Nikola Tesla, whose work formed the basis for the modern alternating current (AC) electrical motor.

The 2008 Ferrari California revives the name first used with the 250GT in 1957 and is the first front-engined Ferrari to be equipped with a V-8 engine. Designed by Pininfarina to be a multi-role sports 2+2, the California features a retractable hardtop—another first for Ferrari—and was penned to look as good with the roof up as down. Under its hood is the 90-degree 4.3-liter V-8 developed with Maserati and previously seen in 4.7-liter form in the Alfa Romeo 8C. The crankshaft is designed crossplane to give the exhaust note a very throaty burble. Seven speeds are on offer via the new dual-clutch transmission—a semi-automatic gearbox operated by broad paddles behind the steering wheel.

The new Ferrari's design echoes the 1957 California with its shallow bonnet vent and stylish flowing bodywork. Many hours in the wind tunnel paid off as designers crafted the new

California into the most aerodynamic Ferrari ever built. With brand-new multi-link suspension, the ride and handling are excellent. The interior is luxurious leather and plenty of room is available in the cabin, with two jump seats behind and connecting flaps to the trunk allowing two sets of golf clubs to be stowed. Starting the car via a red button on the steering wheel frees the driver to ponder an awesome 0-to-60-mile-per-hour time of under four seconds.

FERRARI CALIFORNIA

Country of manufacture: Italy
Years of production: 2008–present
Engine: 4,297cc V-8
Output: 450 horsepower
Top speed: 193 miles per hour
Number built: approximately 5,000 through 2010

Did You Know?

Ferrari believes that the California, built on a new production line in Maranello, Italy, will make up 50 percent of all of Ferraris sold in the next few years.

Holland-based Spyker originally built horse-drawn carriages in the late 1800s and began making cars in 1899. The company was highly innovative; its 60HP racer, built in 1903, had several features never seen before in an automobile: it was the first car with a six-cylinder engine, the first with four-wheel-drive, and the first with brakes on all four wheels. Sadly, the original company went out of business in the 1920s, but a new one was launched in 2000 using the same name and building on the marque's heritage.

SPYKER C8 SPYDER

Country of manufacture: The Netherlands
Years of production: 2000–present
Engine: Audi 4.2-liter all-alloy quad-cam V-8
Output: 400–600 horsepower
Top speed: 186–199 miles per hour
Number built: Approximately 252 through 2010

The new Spyker Cars produces fantastically expensive hand-built sports cars based around the Audi 4.2-liter, 40-valve, all-alloy

quad-cam V-8. Mated to a six-speed manual transmission, the tuned powerplant delivers up to 600 horsepower. The styling is striking and not to everyone's taste—with vents and ducts all over the place and an interior of polished aluminum and embossed leather—but it certainly is eye-catching. Since its rebirth, Spyker has demonstrated a commitment to racing, competing regularly at Le Mans and Sebring, and is in the process developing its sporting brand and raising its profile in the global market.

Did You Know?

In 1914, the original Spyker company merged with the Dutch aircraft factory NV and introduced the propeller to its badge design. The company also coined its motto, "For the tenacious, no road is impassable." Given how treacherous roads were in those early days of the automobile, this was an ambitious statement.

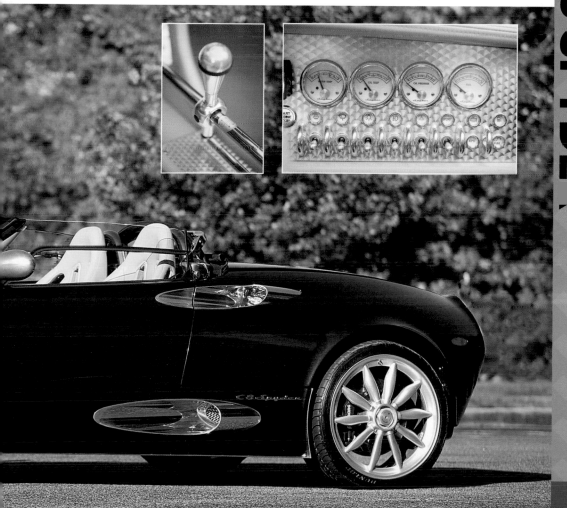

The smart brand (the "s" is always lowercase) was originally conceived by Nicolas Hayek, CEO of the famous Swatch company, who believed that there was a market for an economical city car. He would eventually join forces with Mercedes-Benz, and the result was the first smart car, called the fortwo, which arrived in 1998. It was just 98 inches long and featured radical engineering, including a "safety shell" made of Tridion steel in lieu of a traditional chassis and a rear-mounted three-cylinder motor.

SMART ROADSTER

Country of manufacture: Germany
Years of production: 2003–2006
Engine: 698cc turbocharged three-cylinder
Output: 101 horsepower (Brabus-tuned version)
Top speed: 108 miles per hour (estimated)
Number built: 43,091

The smart roadster and roadster coupe were introduced at the 2002 Paris Motor Show. Both are equipped with a turbocharged inline three-cylinder Suprex engine that produces more than

85 horsepower. Built on a stretched platform, the roadsters are much smaller than any other car in their range but pack remarkably good performance and great fuel efficiency. Available with an electric soft hood and a hard Targa-style roof panel, the little sports car does not have a good reputation for being water tight.

In 2008, smart began offering a limited-edition run of cars prepped by German tuner Brabus. These models, such as the one shown here, featured an engine upgraded to over 100 horsepower, twin exhausts, a higher trim level, lower suspension, and a semi-automatic sequential gearbox operated via Formula 1–type gear paddles behind the steering wheel.

Did You Know?

The ultimate smart roadster prototype was built by Brabus and featured two three-cylinder engines joined together to make a V-6. With twin turbochargers, it kicked out more than 215 horsepower. Just 16 were made and they never went on sale to the general public.

As with the Mazda MX-5 Miata, much of the design work for the Audi TT was done in California. The concept was first shown at the 1995 Frankfurt Auto Show to great acclaim. Built on the Audi A4 platform, production began at Audi's plant in Gyor, Hungary, in September 1998. The production car looked very much like its concept cousin, a notable difference being the addition of rear quarterlights. The TT was offered in 2+2 coupe and two-seat roadster models, with an inline, transverse, four-cylinder, 20-valve engine at the front, turbocharged to two different boost

AUDI TT

Country of manufacture: Germany
Years of production: 1998–present
Engine: 1.8–3.2-liter four-/five-/six-cylinder engines
Output: 158–335 horsepower
Top speed: 155 miles per hour
Number built: 436,713+

profiles yielding 178 and 222 horsepower. Suspension is independent all around with MacPherson struts.

Audi has offered several upgrades to its landmark roadster over the years. In 2003,

Audi began offering a 247-horsepower 3.2-liter VR-6 (six cylinders offset in two rows, each row tilted at an angle of 10 to 15 degrees) engine for both two-wheel-drive and Quattro models. Two years later, Audi introduced a dual-clutch system called Direct Shift that brought improved acceleration. That same year, a lightweight Quattro Sport arrived with more power from the turbo and a higher top speed of 155 miles per hour.

In 2006, the Mk.II TT appeared (shown here), with aluminum panels at the front of the car and steel at the back. It managed a near-neutral weight balance, ideal for handling performance, and featured a new 1.8-liter engine with the TFSi fuel injection system derived from Audi's highly successful endurance race program. The engine offered more power and greater efficiency. There was also a diesel Quattro model, another link to Audi's incredible Le Mans successes. The most powerful and fastest TT arrived in 2009 beneath Audi's famous RS performance badge.

Did You Know?

There's some conflict as to where the TT name was derived. It appeared on a number of cars in the 1960s from NSU, a motorcycle company that was later merged into Audi. NSU had enjoyed success in the famous Isle of Man TT (Tourist Trophy) motorcycle races. According to other sources, TT on the new Audi stands for "Technology and Tradition."

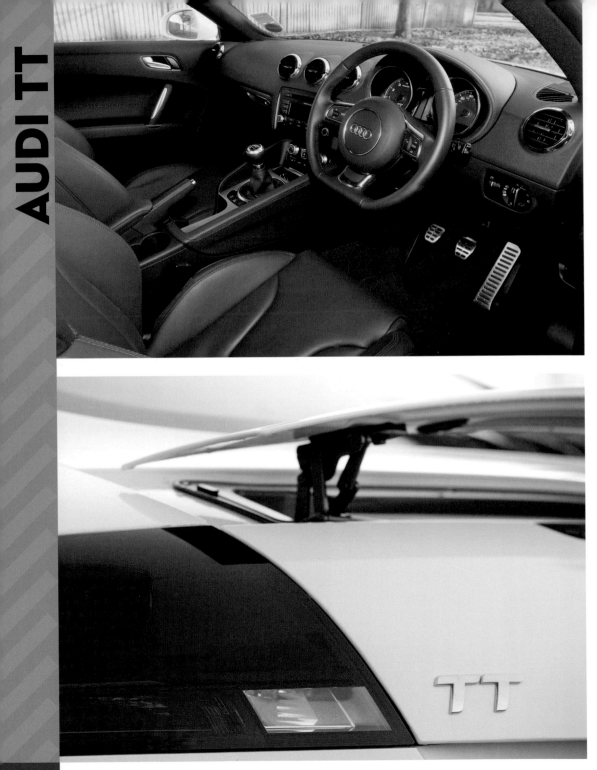

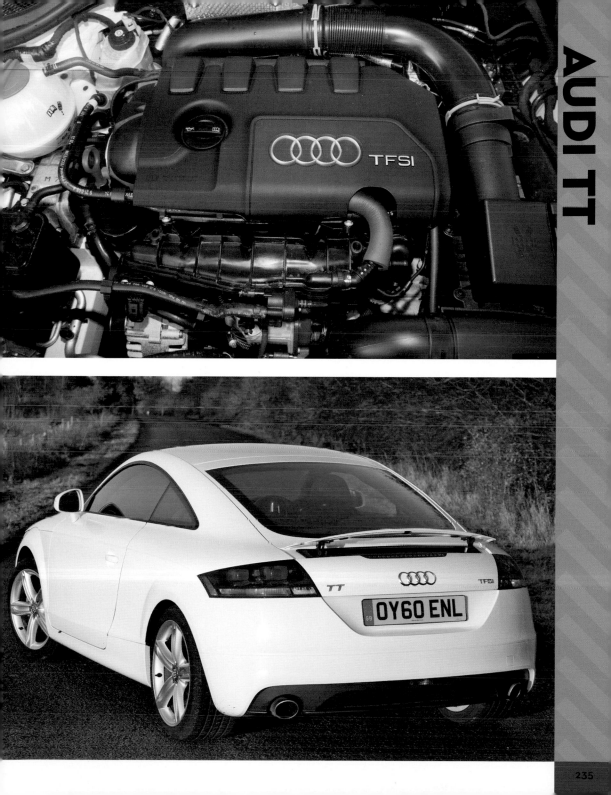

The third generation of the now-classic MX-5 Miata took the model into its 20th year, and it keeps on going as one of the greatest drivers' cars ever made. New, almost retro styling harkened back to the first car that enchanted the world a few decades earlier, but the updated model shared few components with previous models and introduced two brand-new engines. The 1.8-liter and 2.0-liter 16-valve twin-cams were capable of producing 170 horsepower and featured five- or six-speed manual transmission with steering wheel paddle shifters controlling a

MAZDA MX-5 MIATA (THIRD GENERATION)

Country of manufacture: Japan
Years of production: 2005–present
Engine: 1,800–2,000cc 16-valve twin-cam inline four
Output: 170 horsepower
Top speed: 134 miles per hour
Number built: 50,000+

semi-automatic gearbox. New also was the suspension setup, with a multi-link arrangement replacing the double wishbone at

the rear, augmented electronically by traction and stability control.

The third-generation Miata's high point may have come in 2006 in the form of the three-piece retractable hardtop roadster coupe version. In a mere 12 seconds, the roof folds in very neatly behind the seats, leaving the trunk space totally intact. Although it added weight to the car, the retractable hardtop does not affect performance figures badly: Compared to the standard model, the roadster coupe has a higher top speed, although its acceleration dipped slightly from 7.9 to 8.2 seconds on 0-to-60-mile-per-hour runs.

In 2009, a facelift brought a new, more aggressive front with a wider mesh grille and sharper accented headlights.

Did You Know?

In 2009, Mazda commemorated the 20th anniversary of the Miata with the creation of the MX-5 Superlight concept. Designed at the Mazda Frankfurt studio, it was built of various lightweight materials to improve its performance and fuel economy.

INDEX